WORLD WAR I

"The War to End Wars"

Zachary Kent

—American War Series—

ENSLOW PUBLISHERS, INC.

44 Fadem Road	P.O. Box 38
Box 699	Aldershot
Springfield, N.J. 07081	Hants GU12 6BP
U.S.A.	U.K.

> *"This war—as the next war—*
> *was called the war to end wars."*
> —David Lloyd George, quoted on "World War I,"
> PBS on March 28, 1976.

Library of Congress Cataloging-in-Publication Data

Kent, Zachary.
    World War I : the war to end wars / Zachary Kent.
        p. cm. — (American War Series)
    Includes bibliographical references and index.
    ISBN 0-89490-523-6
    1. World War, 1914-1918—Juvenile literature. [1. World War,
1914-1918.] I. Title. II. Title: World War 1. III. Title: World War
One. IV. Series.
    D521.K35 1994
    940.3—dc20   93-46357
                                         CIP
                                         AC
Printed in the United States of America

10 9 8 7 6 5 4

Illustration Credits:
Courtesy of the Prints and Photographs Division, Library of Congress,
p. 11; Earl McElfresh, McElfresh Map Co., pp. 15, 20, 116; National
Archives, pp. 6, 17, 19, 22, 26, 28, 31, 33, 37, 41, 42, 46, 48, 51, 53, 54,
55, 57, 61, 62, 65, 69, 73, 76, 79, 81, 83, 86, 88, 93, 97, 103, 105, 106,
107, 110, 114, 119.

Cover Illustration:
Courtesy of The U.S. Army Art Activity.

Contents

Foreword

At a country auction in upstate New York a few years ago I bought a handsome pair of brass binoculars. They had belonged to a man named G. G. Volkmar. Etched on the brass were the words *U.S. Navy*. Included with the binoculars was a very interesting letter dated May 9, 1918.

> Dear Sir:
> Your prompt and patriotic response to the NAVY's call for binoculars . . . is most appreciated. The glasses will be very useful in the prosecution of Naval Operations until victory is won. . . . On behalf of the NAVY, I wish to thank you most heartily.
>
> Very respectfully,
> Franklin D. Roosevelt
> Assistant Secretary of the Navy

In 1914 war erupted across Europe. The Allied nations of France, Great Britain, and Russia battled against the Central Powers of Germany, Austria-Hungary, and Turkey in what became known as The Great War. When the United States entered the fight on the side of the Allies in 1917, every loyal American citizen wished to pitch in. Mr. Volkmar gladly loaned his binoculars to America's war effort.

When I look at that pair of binoculars now resting on my living-room table, I am reminded of that time. When World War I ended in 1918, 116,000 American soldiers had died of wounds and disease. These men represented only a small number among the millions who perished in World War I. It was a senseless war and a brutal war, more horrible than anyone could have imagined. When it joined the fight, the United States found a national pride that propelled it to international greatness. But in the process America lost its sense of innocence.

NOTICE! Travellers intending to embark on the Atlantic voyage are reminded that a state of war exists between Germany and her allies and Great Britain and her allies; that the zone of war includes the waters adjacent to the British Isles.

—from a warning printed in the *New York Times* by the Imperial German Embassy, May 1, 1915

1 The Sinking of the *Lusitania*

 A long, black German submarine lurked unseen beneath the ocean's surface. Several miles off the southern coast of Ireland, Captain Walther Schwieger raised the periscope of U-boat 20. Peering through the eyepiece, he could hardly believe what he saw. Steaming along some 700 yards away was the great British passenger liner *Lusitania*. The *Lusitania*, the fastest ship on the Atlantic Ocean, weighed 31,550 tons and was 790 feet in length. In Germany's war against Great Britain the sinking of such a target would be a tremendous victory. At just after two o'clock on the afternoon of May 7, 1915, Schwieger ordered, "Fire one!" In the torpedo room a sailor pulled a firing lever. A fierce

hissing swept through the submarine as high-pressure air blasted the torpedo out of its tube.

Aboard the *Lusitania,* passenger Oliver Bernard caught sight of something strange as he gazed out at the bright blue sea. "What is that streak in the water?" he wondered. "It's spreading. It's coming closer."[1] A ship's lookout suddenly noticed the white wake and shouted, "Torpedo coming on the starboard side!" Within seconds, the torpedo crashed into the liner's hull. The explosion sounded like "a million-ton hammer" hitting a giant steel drum, passenger Michael Byrne remembered.

A German U-boat plows through the North Atlantic. German submarines preyed on defenseless British and French cargo and passenger ships during the early years of World War I.

It is not clear whether the second explosion that quickly followed was caused by a cargo of ammunition stowed aboard the _Lusitania_ or by an exploding boiler. The second explosion rocked the ship. On the starboard side, deck planks, lifeboats, coal dust, and water flew upwards. In the dining saloon, fearful first-class passengers scattered from their luncheon tables as the glass from shattered windows and portholes showered them. Elsewhere, the force of the blast knocked people to the floor. Flames and smoke poured into some staterooms and through corridors.

Aboard the German U-20, Captain Schwieger stared through his periscope. "Shot hits starboard side right behind bridge," he noted in his log. "A . . . heavy detonation follows with a very strong explosion cloud."[2]

Already the _Lusitania_ was tilting to starboard and settling deeper into the water. From below, the crew tumbled out onto the boat deck. "Boat stations!" Captain William Turner soon ordered. The crewmen prepared to lower the lifeboats. Alarmed passengers streamed up the companionways or wandered about in confusion. Passengers carrying babies and lifejackets struggled to reach the deck. Many rushed upstairs shirtless or shoeless. Cursing and shrieking, the terrified crowd pressed up against the deck rails. Without engine power, the ship drifted. Tons of seawater poured in through open lower-deck portholes. Passengers trapped inside the ship's electric elevator screamed for help as the water slowly rose about their feet.

Few passengers imagined that such a huge and grand

ship as the *Lusitania* could be sunk quickly by one torpedo. Only minutes had passed since the torpedo had struck. Panicked passengers clung together in helpless masses along the starboard side of the deckhouse. Above them the ship's towering funnels leaned far to one side, and water crept rapidly along the deck from the now almost submerged bow. Passenger Belle Naish realized, "We're sinking fast. It can't be long now."

People scrambled wildly aboard lifeboats. "Lower away!" crewmen yelled. They tried to swing the boats over the rails. Some of the heavy lifeboats broke away, crushing people against the deck. Others dropped awkwardly, spilling their passengers into the water.

The *Lusitania* rolled further to starboard as passengers fought desperately to save themselves. Women cried, "Don't leave us!" When crowded lifeboats could not take them, they flung themselves into the sea. One passenger, American millionaire Alfred Vanderbilt, calmly tried to rescue as many children as he could. He also removed his lifejacket and gave it to a woman without one. He made no attempt to save himself.

Only six lifeboats were successfully launched. There were also twenty-six "collapsibles." These life rafts were made of canvas and wood and were stowed beneath the regular boats. Crewmen cut their lashings in the hope that they would float free. Those in the water tried to find debris to keep themselves afloat. Josephine Brandell caught a deck chair as it floated past her.

Soon the ship's starboard side dipped to its rails. As the bow sank beneath the sea, a great wave of water rushed along the deck, washing people away. Swimming away from the liner, Dr. Carl Foss saw the propellers and rudders plainly visible as the liner went into a slow dive. Two of the huge smokestacks toppled into the water. There was a great, groaning sigh as the water came over them. A last rush of steam sprayed above the funnel tops. The mastheads vanished, and then there was nothing left but the sea. Eighteen minutes after the German torpedo struck, the *Lusitania* had sunk beneath the waves.

During the next hours, Irish fishing boats and tugs hurried to the scene to pluck survivors from the cold sea. On the rescue boats, the survivors huddled under blankets and sipped hot tea as they were brought back to land. The passengers and crew of the *Lusitania* had numbered 1,959. Altogether, 1,198 perished in the disaster, including 270 women and 94 children.

Americans gasped when they heard the news. "American citizens are among the victims," the *New York Tribune* soon exclaimed. There had been 197 Americans on board, and 128 of them had lost their lives.

Many newspapers published a heartbreaking family photograph. It showed Mrs. Paul Crompton of Philadelphia and her six children, all of whom were lost. The brave millionaire Alfred Vanderbilt and other well-known Americans also had drowned. The New York *American* called the German torpedo attack a "deed of wholesale murder." Since 1914 war had raged across Europe. But most Americans bitterly condemned this new type of submarine warfare against defenseless ships. The *New York Times* declared: "From our Department of State there must go to the Imperial Government at Berlin a demand that the Germans shall no longer make war like savages drunk with blood." Colonel Edward M. House, a close advisor to U.S. President Woodrow Wilson, predicted, "We shall be at war with Germany within a month."[3]

But Wilson wished to keep America neutral and out of the war at all costs. In a speech at Convention Hall in Philadelphia three days after the sinking, Wilson proclaimed: "There is such a thing as a man being too proud to fight. There is such a thing as a nation being so right that it does not need to convince others by force that it is right.[4]

Many Americans, however, disagreed. The *New York Times* declared that "this utterance of the President does not respond to the feeling of the people." The *New York World* insisted: "We have a pride that will make us fight." The sympathies of the American people had been split between Britain and Germany until the "Lusitania Massacre." After the ship's sinking, Americans turned their outrage toward Germany. Many began preparing for a war they were sure would come. Manufacturers worked with more energy to supply the Allies. Young men flocked to summer military camps to learn how to be soldiers. Two more years would pass before the United States declared war on Germany. But the sinking of the *Lusitania* made many Americans eager to join the fight.

The New York *World* announces the *Lusitania* disaster on the front page of its May 8, 1915 edition. Below the photograph of the *Lusitania*, a map pinpoints where the liner was sunk off the southern coast of Ireland.

For all we have and are,
For all our children's fate,
Stand up and take the war,
The Hun is at the gate!
—from a poem by British writer Rudyard Kipling

2 The World at War

 In the first fateful days of August 1914 when World War I was beginning, no one could guess that before its end the whole world would be drawn into conflict. Thrones would topple, empires would disappear, and countries would vanish. The world would never be the same again.

The Fatal Shots

Archduke Franz Ferdinand and his wife, Sophie, were being driven in an open automobile through the streets of Sarajevo in Bosnia on June 28, 1914. The fifty-one-year-old archduke, heir to the Hapsburg Empire of Austria-Hungary, was scheduled to attend a review of Austrian troops. The people of Bosnia were Serbs and Croats. Many of them resented being part of the

Hapsburg Empire instead of Serbia, their national state. Several Serbian university students stood in the crowd along the parade route. They planned to use this opportunity to assassinate the hated archduke.

One plotter heaved a bomb at the passing automobile. It landed in the street and exploded, spraying fragments in all directions. The startled archduke remained unhurt. Angrily he ordered the chauffeur to drive straight out of town. The chauffeur, however, took a wrong turn, then stopped the car and reversed. In the roadside crowd, Gavrilo Princip, another of the assassins, jumped onto the running board. He drew a pistol and fired twice. One bullet struck Ferdinand in the neck. The other hit Sophie in the abdomen. Both died almost immediately.

The archduke's assassination shocked Europeans and set off a deadly chain reaction. At the start of the 1900s three cousins, all grandsons of Great Britain's Queen Victoria, ruled three of Europe's largest nations. Wilhelm II sat on the throne as kaiser of Germany, Nicholas II ruled as absolute czar of Russia, and George V wore the crown of king of Great Britain. Since 1870 when Germany first became a united nation, its leaders had desired greater world power. Great Britain and France possessed colonies throughout the world. Germany wished to establish colonies, too. Over the next forty years Germany built up a navy and army, and factories to support them. German navy yards rushed to build ships. The kaiser, on horseback, proudly reviewed new German infantry regiments, and German munitions factories, such as the giant Krupp works, manufactured tons of heavy cannon, artillery, and rifles.

These German efforts to gain increased power worried many Europeans. The assassination of Archduke Ferdinand provided the spark that would touch off a war. Arnold Whitridge, a young American student traveling in Europe in 1914, realized:

> After Archduke Franz Ferdinand was assassinated, you could see the tensions building up everywhere—one thing just seemed to follow another. . . . There hadn't been a major war in Europe for so many years, and everyone seemed to clamor for one.[1]

The Age of Alliances

During the previous twenty years, Europe had formed itself into a confused tangle of political and military alliances, in which one nation pledged to support another. Allied together, the governments of Austria-Hungary and Germany thought they had become very powerful. Archduke Franz Ferdinand's death put the strength of Europe's various alliances to the test.

"Serbia must learn to fear us again," declared Austrian diplomat Wilhelm Ritter von Stork after Ferdinand's assassination. Kaiser Wilhelm II of Germany also advised his Austrian allies to take a strong line. On July 23, the Austro-Hungarian government sent a list of vengeful legal demands to Serbia designed to give Austria-Hungary greater power over that country. When the Serbs failed to meet all of these demands, Austria-Hungary declared war on Serbia on July 28, 1914.

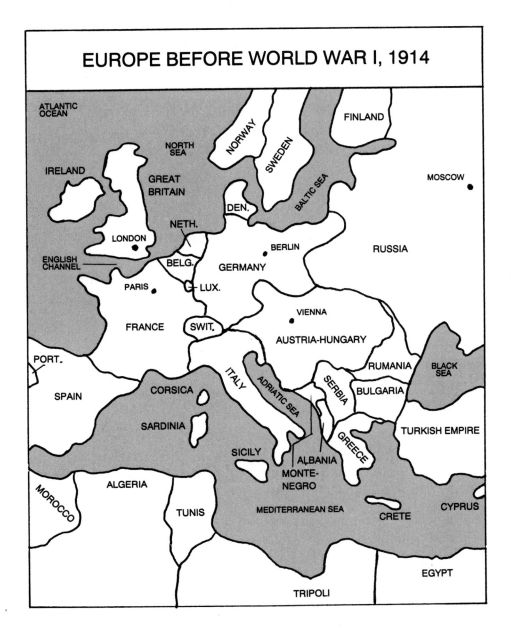

EUROPE BEFORE WORLD WAR I, 1914

ATLANTIC
OCEAN

NORWAY

SWEDEN

FINLAND

NORTH
SEA

BALTIC SEA

MOSCOW

IRELAND

GREAT
BRITAIN

DEN.

NETH.

LONDON

ENGLISH
CHANNEL

BELG.

BERLIN

RUSSIA

GERMANY

PARIS

LUX.

VIENNA

FRANCE

SWIT.

AUSTRIA-HUNGARY

PORT.

ITALY

ADRIATIC SEA

RUMANIA

BLACK
SEA

SPAIN

CORSICA

SERBIA

BULGARIA

SARDINIA

TURKISH EMPIRE

SICILY

ALBANIA

GREECE

MONTE-
NEGRO

MOROCCO

ALGERIA

CYPRUS

TUNIS

MEDITERRANEAN SEA

CRETE

EGYPT

TRIPOLI

Austria-Hungary had Germany as an ally, but Serbia had Russia. On July 30, Czar Nicholas II ordered Russia's armies to prepare for war. German diplomats demanded that Russia halt its plans at once. The Russians refused, and on August 1, 1914, Germany declared war on Russia. Two days later Germany declared war on France, another Russian ally. World War I began because statesmen foolishly thought they could bully one another with threats.

On August 2, Germany demanded free passage through Belgium in order to attack France. The Belgians refused, and this refusal brought Belgium's ally Great Britain into the war. Germany was already wheeling 1,500,000 soldiers into line toward France. Another 500,000 were mobilized to face eastward toward Russia. Across Europe more than six million soldiers were getting marching orders. Troop trains with whistles screaming rolled out of railroad stations. People crowded the streets in every capital, excitedly yelling "to Paris" or "to Berlin."

The Western Front

"You will be home before the leaves have fallen from the trees," Kaiser Wilhelm told his departing troops. Germany's military Schlieffen Plan called for the German armies to march through the Low Countries of Belgium and Luxembourg and invade France from the weakly defended north. A young lieutenant commanded the lead company of the German 69th Infantry Regiment that crossed the Luxembourg border at 7:00 P.M. on August

A German cavalry regiment proudly parades through Berlin in August 1914. Nearly 60,000 soldiers such as these spearheaded the German invasion into Belgium.

1, 1914, and captured the railway station at the village of
Ulflingen. Within twenty-four hours, Luxembourg was
fully occupied. German general Erich Ludendorff captured the key Belgian city of Liege by battering it to
pieces with heavy howitzer fire during a ten-day siege.
Elsewhere the German advance was even more swift and
brutal.

"Frightened civilians lined the streets," German lieutenant Fritz Nagel remembered, "hands held high as a
sign of surrender. Bedsheets hung out of windows for the
same purpose. To see those frightened men, women and
children was a really terrible sight."

British newspapers printed horror stories of the German march through Belgium. Articles told of Belgian
girls and women tortured and murdered and of children
stabbed with bayonets and trampled beneath the hooves
of German cavalry horses. Mobs of panicked Belgians
crowded the dusty roads, fleeing the German advance.
The British compared the Germans to the hordes of
Huns who had swarmed through Europe in the Middle
Ages.

The Third and Fourth armies of France counterattacked eastward from the province of Lorraine on August
14. The offensive shattered when it came up against
strong fortifications at the German border. At the same
time, a British army of 100,000 soldiers commanded by
Sir John French crossed the English Channel and took
up a position near the Belgian border at Mons, France.
On August 22, a British pilot reported seeing field-gray

German columns rolling toward the twenty-seven-mile British front.

At Mons on August 23, 1914, two British divisions of 35,000 men held off four German army corps totalling more than 160,000 men. British rifle fire cut down the charging Germans in rows. British corporal W. Holbrook recalled, "You'd see a lot of them coming in a mass . . . and you just let them have it. They kept retreating, and then coming forward, and then retreating again." Heavily outnumbered, by day's end the British had to retreat. "The position was hopeless," British lieutenant K.F.B. Tower later declared. "We darted off

British troops advance toward the front. After the bloody fighting at Mons, France, on August 23, 1914, British lieutenant E.H.T. Broadwood recalled, "We lay under . . . shellfire for three hours and I think that none of us will ever forget the feeling of thinking that the next moment we might be dead—perhaps blown to atoms."

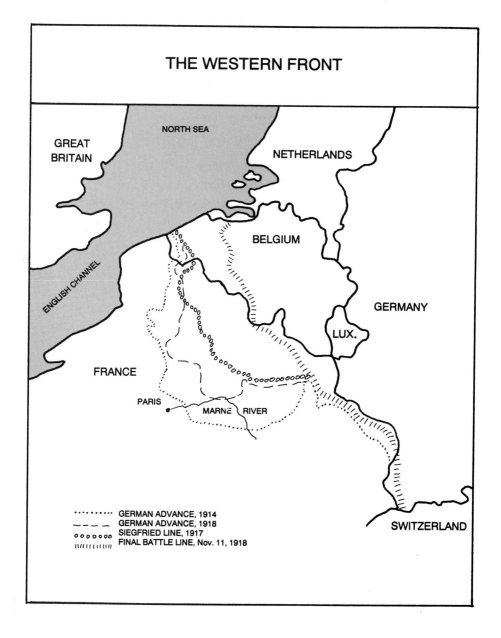

THE WESTERN FRONT

GREAT
BRITAIN

NORTH SEA

NETHERLANDS

ENGLISH CHANNEL

BELGIUM

GERMANY

LUX.

FRANCE

PARIS

MARNE RIVER

SWITZERLAND

.... GERMAN ADVANCE, 1914
− − − − GERMAN ADVANCE, 1918
o o o o o o o SIEGFRIED LINE, 1917
ιιιιιιιιιιιι FINAL BATTLE LINE, Nov. 11, 1918

under a hail of fire and I don't know how on earth we got away."[2]

After knocking the British out of his path, commanding German general Helmuth von Moltke ordered a major change in the Schlieffen Plan. Now the Germans turned southwest and marched toward Paris. On September 2, a German biplane dropped propaganda leaflets over Paris with the message: "There is nothing you can do but surrender." As the Germans crossed the Marne River, fifty miles from Paris, French general Joseph Joffre called for a desperate French counterattack. "Soldiers of France," he sternly commanded, "we are attacking. Advance as long as you can. When you can no longer advance, hold your position. When you can no longer hold it, die."

For seven days, Germans and Frenchmen recklessly attacked each other all along the Western Front. On the huge battlefield of the Marne, both sides fell in bloody waves. When the French weakened at one point along the line on September 8, French general Joseph Gallieni collected some 1,200 taxicabs in Paris and rushed in several thousand reinforcements to save the position. Known as the "Miracle of the Marne," this movement helped turn the tide against the Germans. On September 14, the exhausted Germans pulled back to the Aisne River. They scratched holes in the ground and set up machine guns. The enemy armies now glared at one another from the safety of opposing networks of defensive ditches. Trench warfare had begun. The war of movement had ended.

The Eastern Front

In August 1914, only 135,000 soldiers defended Germany's eastern border in Prussia. With surprising speed, 650,000 Russian soldiers, commanded by the Grand Duke Nicholas, uncle of the czar, marched against that line. At Gumbinnen on August 20, the Russians overwhelmed the enemy and threatened to overrun East

General Paul von Hindenburg (left) and General Erich Ludendorff (right) plot strategy with Kaiser Wilhelm II at German General Headquarters. On the Eastern Front at Tannenberg at the end of August 1914, the Germans scored a stunning victory and sent their Russian enemies reeling backward.

Prussia (present-day Poland). In this German emergency, sixty-seven-year-old General Paul Von Hindenburg was brought out of retirement and named new commander of the German Eighth Army.

On August 29, the Germans attacked around the city of Tannenberg in East Prussia along a sixty-mile front. The Masurian Lakes created a wide gap between two major Russian armies. The Germans attacked first one army and then the other. In four days 90,000 Russian prisoners were taken. Broken Russian divisions fell back in disorder. The Battle of Tannenberg cleared German territory and made Hindenburg a German national hero.

In the fall of 1914, the Germans pushed eastward into Poland. On December 6, the Germans captured the city of Lodz. In March 1915, the Tenth Russian Army was destroyed in the Polish forest of Augustow. The whole Russian army was poorly trained and equipped. In battle, many unarmed troops had to snatch rifles from the hands of their dead comrades. As their battleline broke apart, the Russians abandoned most of Poland. On August 5, the Russians evacuated the city of Warsaw in a general retreat. By the end of August of 1915 the Russians had lost 750,000 men as prisoners alone, and more territory than the whole of France. German general Erich Ludendorff commented, "We had taken a great step toward Russia's overthrow."

Further south in Galicia, in Austria-Hungary, vast hordes of Russians and Serbs smashed an Austrian army.

By November of 1914, the Russians reached the Carpathian Mountains leading into Hungary. In the spring of 1915, the Germans aided the Austrians in a furious counterattack. On May 2, they captured the city of Tarnow and continued smashing the Russians along a 250-mile front, capturing 150,000 prisoners.

Faced with disaster, Czar Nicholas II dismissed his uncle as the Russian army's Commander-in-Chief. On September 5, 1915, the Czar announced, "Today I have taken supreme command of all forces of the sea and land armies operating in the theater of war. We shall fulfill our sacred duty to defend our country to the last."[3]

The last gasp of the Russian Army occurred in June 1916. An attack commanded by Russian general Aleksei Brusilov crushed the Austrian defenses over a 200-mile front along the Rumanian frontier. The Austrian Fourth and Seventh armies collapsed. Once more the Russians almost reached the Carpathian Mountains. The Austrians lost more than 600,000 men, some 400,000 of them being captured. But Brusilov had paid a high price. One million Russians—the army's best and most loyal soldiers—were killed or wounded. The shaken survivors were ripe for revolution.

Deadlock on the Western Front

"The lull during the winter has allowed each side on this front to fortify itself so strongly that, in my opinion, the deadlock here is permanent," American volunteer Alan Seeger, serving in the British army, wrote to his mother.

By the end of 1914, the Western Front stretched

through northeastern France from the English Channel some 470 miles to Switzerland.

The battleline had grown into a complicated network of trenches. No one was prepared for this kind of warfare. Soldiers attacked and counterattacked across the open ground, charging straight into bunched machine-gun fire and volleying rifles. At the First Battle of Ypres the previous fall, Germany had lost 130,000 soldiers. By January of 1915, the British in France had lost 90 percent of its army. "This isn't war!" cried Britain's Field-Marshal Earl Kitchener in shock.[4]

Advances in military technology caused much of the bloodshed. Soldiers filled with the romance of war were stunned by rapid-firing machine guns, flamethrowers, and artillery shells that could destroy a whole village in a matter of minutes. Barbed wire lay over acres and acres of ground between the enemy lines, making charges nearly impossible.

German scientists also developed chemical warfare. Poison chlorine gas was first used at Ypres on April 22, 1915. During a mortar barrage the heavier-than-air poison rolled into the Allied trenches like a greenish-yellow fog, bringing death, shock, and panic. British sergeant Bill Hay described it.

> Of course, the chaps were all gasping and couldn't breathe, and it was ghastly . . . terrible for a wounded man to lie there! The gasping, the gasping! And . . . your eyes were stinging as well. You couldn't stop to help anybody, even if he was your brother.

Later, phosgene gas proved twice as deadly as chlorine. Soon all troops were wearing protective gas masks. Over the course of the war, gas caused over 79,000 deaths.

At the war's start every army possessed a few airplanes that were used for purposes of scouting. The Germans, however, started to bomb England in 1915. This was done at first with huge inflated airships called zeppelins. In 1916 the Germans also began using biplanes for their bombing raids. Although only 1,100 English people died in the air attacks, the raids always caused fear and confusion.

French soldiers spray liquid fire at their enemy. Flamethrowers, poison gas, barbed wire, and machine guns joined the list of horrible new weapons used in World War I.

The Germans had one other device that turned out to be very dangerous. This was the U-boat or submarine. The Germans declared a sea blockade of the British Isles early in 1915. U-boats sank enemy ships on sight, leaving crews and passengers to drown.

At the end of 1915, Sir Douglas Haig was named new commander of the British army in France, while Marshal Joffre still commanded the French troops. The Germans adjusted to trench warfare faster than the British or the French. When French soldiers attacked at Champagne, France, on September 25, 1915, they overran the German front line. But they discovered, to their surprise, that the Germans had prepared a second stronger line 200 yards behind it. This line contained deep trenches, underground dugouts, and concrete strong points called pillboxes. This new trench system turned ordinary offensives into pointless slaughters.

Veteran troops learned to remain in their trenches as much as possible. They sloshed through knee-deep mud, while rats and roaches plagued their dugout sleeping quarters. Soldiers' clothes became thick with lice (called "cooties"). "We are not leading the life of men at all," declared British volunteer Alan Seeger, "but that of animals, living in holes in the ground, and only showing outside to fight and to feed."

The Global Conflict

As imperialist nations, Britain and France called upon their far-flung colonies to fill the trenches of France. The British Commonwealth nations of Canada, Australia,

A German pilot drops a bomb. It is not surprising that with such
crude bombing methods few bombs hit their targets.

and New Zealand loyally contributed troops. So did British colonial India. Algerians, Senegalese, Moroccans, and Vietnamese troops answered the French call for help. British colonial troops in Africa quickly conquered German Southwest Africa as well as Germany's other African colonies. In remote East Asia, Japan entered the war in August 1914 as Great Britain's ally. Japanese troops captured the German colonial port of Tsingtao in China on October 31, 1914. The Great War, the first truly world war, now stretched from one end of the globe to the other.

In October 1914, the Ottoman Empire of Turkey, led by Talaat Pasha and Enver Pasha, entered the war on the German side. Moslem Turks used the war as an excuse to massacre the Christian Armenians and Greeks within their empire. More than two million innocent people were slaughtered or enslaved.

Bulgaria joined the Central Powers in October 1914 and then invaded Serbia. On October 5, 1915, one British and one French division landed at the port of Salonika in neutral Greece. Despite being unable to press northward into the Balkans against the Germans, Austrians, and Bulgarians, the British and French still sent more than 500,000 men to Salonika by the end of the war.

On May 23, 1915, Italy declared war against Austria-Hungary. The campaign in Italy became a series of useless battles. Fighting eleven times at Isonzo, the Italians could not shake the hold of the Austrians on their mountain barrier. Rumania in turn declared war on

Austria on August 27, 1916. As a result, the Rumanians suffered stunning defeats at the hands of the Austrians and the Germans.

First Lord of the Admiralty Winston Churchill assured the British government that the Royal Navy could capture the Dardanelles, the important Turkish strait leading from the Mediterranean Sea to the Black Sea. On February 19, 1915, British and French warships began bombarding the Turkish forts at the Dardanelles. Soon, however, two British battleships and one French battleship struck mines and sank. The naval attack was called off. Instead, Britain's Lord Horatio Kitchener sent out General Sir Ian Hamilton with orders to capture Turkey's Gallipoli Peninsula, saying, "If you do, you will have won not only a campaign, but the war."

Hamilton landed 70,000 British troops on April 25, 1915. They included two divisions of the Australia–New Zealand Army Corps (ANZACS). Australian captain T. A. White remembered,

> At 4:30 P.M. we dropped anchor off Anzac Cove. On all sides battleships were bombarding the distant hills; nearer in towards the shore were transports discharging their troops into destroyers, which then darted towards the shore to discharge the men into rowing boats. Shells were bursting around and over the vessels and boats and we could hear the crackling of machine guns and rifles.

"There were lines of men clinging like cockroaches under the cliffs," recalled Irish captain Aubrey Herbert.

Australian troops charge a Turkish trench on Gallipoli. The
Australia-New Zealand Army Corps (ANZACs) suffered brutally
during Allied attempts to capture that key Turkish peninsula.

"The only thing to be done was to dig in as soon as possible, but a good many men were shot while they were doing this." The British troops were pinned down on the rocky shore, unable to reach the top of the hills and move into open country. There was no shade. Everything, even water, had to be landed at night. New Zealander private Leonard Hart declared,

> During these days our losses had been very heavy and a number of our men had been taken bad with . . . fever. The smell of the bodies was becoming intolerable and the flies swarmed in the millions. When a man was killed in the trenches all that could be done was to throw him up on the parapet and leave him until we could spare time at night to bury him.[5]

On August 6, 1915, the British landed five more divisions on Gallipoli, at Anzac Bay and at Sulva Bay. Though they surprised the Turks, the British failed to press their advantage. Finally, after eight months of stalemate, the British evacuated the peninsula in January of 1916. At Gallipoli they had lost 250,000 men including those killed, wounded, and missing. The Turks also suffered some 250,000 casualties.

The Battle of Jutland was the only major engagement of the British and German fleets during the war. The Imperial German Navy challenged the British Royal Navy for control of the seas. Sailors fought the battle on May 31, 1916, about sixty miles west of the Danish coast of Jutland. Commanded by Admiral Sir John Jellicoe, the British had twenty-eight dreadnoughts (battleships), nine battle cruisers, and assorted other ships. The Germans, led by Admiral Reinhard Scheer, had twenty-two dreadnoughts and five battle cruisers, among its fleet. In all, 250 vessels steamed into combat. Cannon-fire flashed across the sea beginning at 6 P.M. The fighting ended late in the night, when the Germans, under the cover of darkness and fog, made their escape. The British lost three battle cruisers, three armored cruisers, and eight destroyers. German losses included the battle cruiser *Lutzow*, the battleship *Pommern*, four light cruisers, and four destroyers. The Battle of Jutland forced the German fleet to remain inside its harbors for

German battleships steam into the North Sea. After losses at the Battle of Jutland on May 31, 1916, the Germans kept their big ships safely anchored inside home harbors. Instead they relied more heavily on the menace of their submarines to fight the war at sea.

the rest of the war. As a result, submarines became the German navy's greatest weapon.

In the Middle East, Turkey kept the British occupied. The British wished to protect the Suez Canal in Egypt and their oil wells in Persia (present-day Iran). In time 600,000 British soldiers were engaged in Mesopotamia (present-day Iraq) and 500,000 more in Palestine.

In 1916, British colonel T. E. Lawrence helped Arab forces under Sheik Faisal al Husein revolt against the Turks on the Arabian Peninsula (present-day Saudi Arabia). Dressed in Arab clothes, "Lawrence of Arabia" led attacks against the Turkish Hejaz railroad and urged the Arab forces under Faisal to cooperate with the British general Sir Edmund Allenby.

"I'd like you to take Jerusalem as a Christmas present for the nation," British Prime Minister David Lloyd George told General Allenby in June 1917. Allenby obliged. After capturing Beersheba, the British lay siege to Jerusalem. The city surrendered on December 9. By late 1918 Colonel Lawrence and General Allenby were operating together, pushing north on parallel routes through the Holy Land toward the city of Damascus. Earlier, in Mesopotamia, 400,000 British soldiers commanded by General Sir Stanley Maude had marched up the Tigris River and captured Baghdad in March 1917.

They Shall Not Pass

"The German Army, when it moves to attack, stops for no obstacle," the Kaiser's son Crown Prince Rupprecht announced on the Western Front at the start of 1916.

General Erich von Falkenhayn of Germany wished to destroy the will of France to fight. He chose the famous fortress at Verdun, on the Meuse River in northern France, as the place to rob the French of their pride. The German buildup of nearly a thousand heavy guns included thirteen 420-millimeter mortars (called "Big Berthas") that threw one-ton projectiles. On February 21, 1916, across a six-mile front the Germans threw two million shells into the forts and trenches of Verdun. The shells rained down at the rate of 200,000 an hour.

Crown Prince Rupprecht's Fifth German Army led the assault that followed. The French defenses east of the Meuse River began to sag. French marshal Henri Philippe Pétain took command at Verdun and solemnly vowed, "They shall not pass." The French possessed a single road leading to the front. Trucks carried 27,000 tons of ammunition and supplies and 190,000 reinforcements along this crucial road, called "The Sacred Way."

The fighting at Verdun was gruesome. A French lieutenant wrote, "What scenes of horror and carnage! . . . Hell cannot be so terrible." American ambulance driver Robert Lowell Moore later declared, "The poor devils, we'd just load them in the ambulance and head for the hospital, over and over again." The French held Verdun, but by the end of June they had lost some 500,000 soldiers, and the Germans had lost more than 400,000.

Just as the fighting ended at Verdun, it flared up between the British and the Germans along the Somme River farther north in the province of Picardy. The Battle of the Somme opened with five days of heavy British bombardment on an eighteen-mile front. Of the shelling, British captain R.J. Trousdell remembered, "Thickly timbered woods were reduced to a few gaunt and splintered trunks. . . . Villages disappeared as though they had never been."

On July 1, 1916, thirteen British divisions, about 200,000 men, went forward together. Climbing "over the top" of their trenches the troops started across No-Man's-Land. The Germans swiftly emerged from their dugouts and manned their machine guns. Into a steady spray of bullets the first British line went. It faltered and fell, a second followed it, a third, and then a fourth, all to no avail. "We never got anywhere near the Germans," British corporal W. H. Shaw later exclaimed. "Never got anywhere near them. . . . The machine-guns . . . were mowing the top of the trenches. You daren't put your finger up. The men were just falling back in the trenches."[6] On that gory July day, 20,000 British soldiers died, the heaviest loss suffered in a single day by any army in World War I.

British general Sir Douglas Haig continued the hopeless fight day after day. During one attack three divisions of cavalry made a charge. With bugles blowing and lances glittering, men and horses were mowed down as the German machine guns opened fire. Tragically these mounted troops learned there was no place for cavalry in modern trench warfare.

In desperation Haig tried a new weapon: the tank. Hidden under canvas during its secret development, this machine was called a "water carrier" or "water tank"

Canadian troops climb "over the top" and charge across No-Man's-Land in 1916. Brave junior officers often led the way. As a result, Allied officers died six times more often than enlisted men.

soon shortened to "tank." Tank designers enclosed cater-
pillar tractors inside fully armored cabins. On September
5, 1916, Haig threw forty-two of them into his attack.
British private Charles Cole watched one of the strange
machines:

> Eventually, the tank got going and went past us.
> The Germans ran for their lives—couldn't make
> out what was firing at them. . . . the tank went on,
> knocked brick walls, houses down, did what it was
> supposed to have done—but too late! We lost
> thousands and thousands . . .

Haig finally called off the fighting on November 18,
1916. The Somme campaign was a dreadful failure. The
British had advanced no more than five miles, and some
420,000 men had been killed or wounded.

The Hindenburg Line

New men and new methods set the scene on the West-
ern Front for 1917. British Lord Kitchener drowned at
sea when the warship *Hampshire* struck a mine and sank
off the Orkney Islands on June 5, 1916. General Sir
William Robertson took over as Supreme Director of
Strategy for the British. When Joseph Joffre was named
Marshal of France, General Robert Nivelle became
French commander of the Western Front. In August
1916, Hindenburg took over in the West as Chief of the
German General Staff with General Erich Ludendorff as
First Quartermaster General.

Ludendorff soon decided to simplify the German
line. Through the winter of 1916–1917, the Germans

prepared a new "Hindenburg Line," carefully chosen for its advantages. Dugouts were constructed and equipped. Concrete positions were built for machine guns. Falling back into this line, Ludendorff could successfully defend his territory with fewer soldiers.

The British began 1917 with an attack at Arras, France, on April 9. British rifleman Ralph Langley described the scene:

> It went on snowing all the time we were advancing. Off we went, and just as we got up to the wire the Germans got me through the leg with a bullet. A rifle bullet. You could see them firing at us. And there were machine-guns going too. . . . I don't know what the Generals wanted to do that attack for, because it was murder.

The fight cost 150,000 British casualties and gained little.

The French also staged an attack that spring. "We will win it all," General Nivelle insisted, "within twenty-four to forty-eight hours."[7] The "Nivelle system," of which he was so proud, called for a swift concentration of troops across the Aisne River. On April 16, Nivelle attacked with three entire French armies, totalling some 1,200,000 men. The guns thundered. The whistles blew. French infantry masses slogged forward in a storm of rain and snow that turned the ground to mud. German artillery showered death on their heads. By evening, the French had gained six hundred yards, not the six miles Nivelle had promised. The trenches and concrete shelters of the Hindenburg Line still frowned in the distance.

Nivelle continued the hopeless attack for another ten days. The French lost more than 200,000 men along the Aisne. The French troops by now were completely disgusted with their generals. One frustrated regiment marched to the front bleating like sheep being led to the slaughter. On April 29, 1917, mutiny broke out in another French regiment. More widespread mutiny followed. Thousands of troops rioted, threw down their rifles, and refused to obey their officers. Many French soldiers deserted their stations. Great stretches of front were left undefended.

General Pétain quickly stepped in to restore order out of chaos. Over 100,000 soldiers were court-martialed. Military courts found 23,000 guilty. Of those, 432 were sentenced to death and 55 were executed. The French soldiers returned to the trenches. But three years of brutal war had broken their spirit completely.

Russia Bows Out

The year 1917 shook the heart of Russia as well. Throughout the previous year, the Russians suffered severe losses along the Eastern Front. On June 4, 1916, General Aleksey Brusilov's Russian army simply attacked at twenty different points, hoping to crack the enemy battleline. The Russians took 250,000 prisoners on the Austro-Hungarian front. But the Germans struck back, forcing Brusilov to retreat. In the end, the Russians suffered over one million casualties in the campaign. To fill its empty ranks the Russian army dragged peasants off their farms. Without farmers to grow crops, Russian marketplaces became bare of food. The masses turned against the Czar, blaming him for their defeats. Hungry Russian soldiers at the front angrily chanted "Bread and Peace." Russian revolutionaries, called Bolsheviks, added a demand for "Land."

Finally, food riots broke out in Petrograd (present-day St. Petersburg), which was then the Russian capital. On March 11, 1917, police using machine guns killed more than two hundred demonstrators in street fighting. The local army garrison mutinied after being ordered to

French troops attack a German position in 1917. The French soldier at the center of the picture has been shot and is about to fall to the ground. Such hopeless charges broke the spirit of the French army.

An unshaven French soldier rests in a dugout behind the lines. French soldiers were commonly known as "poilus" meaning "the hairy ones."

support the police. Instead the soldiers joined in the looting of stores and warehouses. Russian government official Mikhail Rodzianko anxiously wired the Czar: "Anarchy reigns in the capital."

At his military headquarters, Czar Nicholas II seemed powerless. As his empire crumbled around him, the Czar's generals advised him to abdicate. On March 26, Czar Nicholas II signed a paper giving up his throne. The dynasty of the Romanovs was now ended. Workers and soldiers swiftly grabbed control of the government in Petrograd. Calling themselves a council or "soviet," they set up a provisional government of liberal politicians. Alexander Kerensky took the lead in the new government's affairs. At first there was no talk of quitting the war.

One man thought differently, however. This was Nikolai Lenin, the Bolshevik leader who was in exile in Zurich, Switzerland. Lenin (his real name was Vladimir Ilich Ulyanov) was not interested in defeating the Germans. He wanted to establish a socialist government in Russia. Lenin determined to return to Russia at once to take advantage of the turmoil. Ludendorff, eager to weaken Russia, let Lenin pass through Germany on a special train. Lenin arrived in Petrograd on April 16, 1917. He was showered with bouquets of roses by waiting comrades. Lenin at once denounced the Provisional Government and began to preach a new revolution. "What do you get from war?" he asked street crowds. "Only wounds, starvation, and death."

On the Eastern Front, the Russian army was falling

apart. In July 1917, the Russian soldiers lurched against the German lines one last time. After that, disheartened Russian soldiers simply began to quit fighting. Thousands filled the roads heading eastward, toward home. In October, rebellious regiments stationed in Petrograd announced: "We no longer recognize the Provisional Government." Kerensky left Petrograd on November 7, 1917, never to return. That evening Bolshevik volunteers called "Red Guards" captured the Winter Palace and arrested the remaining members of the Provisional Government. Only six Red Guards died in the Bolshevik revolution that brought Lenin to power.

Bolshevik leader Leon Trotsky met with German officials at Brest Litovsk in February 1918. Trotsky proposed a military truce between Russia and Germany. With no enemy in front of them, however, the Germans instead marched onward, taking hundreds of miles of Russian territory. At last, Russia agreed to sign a peace on any terms the Germans offered. On March 3, 1918, Russia signed the treaty of Brest Litovsk, in which they gave up Lithuania, Latvia, Estonia, Poland, and the Ukraine. "This is a peace that Russia, grinding her teeth, is forced to accept," Trotsky bitterly declared.[8] With the fighting now ended on the Eastern Front, Germany turned its full attention westward.

Over there, over there,
Send the word, send the word over there,
That the Yanks are coming, the Yanks are coming,
The drums rum-tumming ev'ry where.
So prepare, say a pray'r,
Send the word, send the word to beware,
We'll be over, we're coming over,
And we won't come back till it's over over there.

—From the 1917 American song "Over There"
by George M. Cohan

3 The Yanks Are Coming

 "He Kept Us Out of War," was the campaign slogan that helped U.S. President Woodrow Wilson win reelection in 1916. In fact, America prospered because of the war. American farmers sold wheat, cotton, and other crops to both the Allies and the Central Powers. American factories sold guns, ammunition, and other war supplies to both sides. Peace-loving Americans sang a popular song entitled, "I Didn't Raise My Boy to Be a Soldier." The United States remained neutral in feelings until the Germans began sinking merchant ships.

Safe For Democracy

When a German torpedo sank the passenger liner *Lusitania* on May 17, 1915, Americans in great numbers

45

suddenly began to favor the Allies. Some fiery young Americans joined the French Foreign Legion. Others slipped over the border into Canada and joined the British royal forces. About two hundred adventurous Americans flew with the French air force. The American Red Cross, the Norton-Harjes, and the American Field Service provided volunteer ambulance drivers to aid wounded British and French forces.

After promising to stop its unrestricted submarine warfare, Germany began it again in January 1917. All shipping in the Atlantic war zone would be sunk on

A vessel torpedoed by a German U-boat sinks beneath the waves. An escaping man slides down a rope as a lifeboat pulls away. Such ruthless attacks helped the United States make its decision to declare war against Germany in April 1917.

sight, Germany said. President Wilson swiftly reacted, breaking diplomatic relations with Germany. Later he released to the public the contents of a German message that had recently been intercepted by the British Secret Service. The "Zimmerman telegram" revealed a plan by the German secretary of state to draw Mexico into war against the United States.

In March 1917, German submarines sank three American ships. War fever heightened throughout the United States. Ex-president Theodore Roosevelt thundered, "There is no question about going to war. Germany is already at war with us." People marched in preparedness parades in cities across the country, carrying banners that read: "Kill the Kaiser!" "On to Berlin!" and "Let's Get the Hun!"

Finally, President Wilson called for a special session of Congress. On the warm, rainy night of April 2, 1917, spectators jammed the galleries of the U.S. House of Representatives. Many congressmen wore small American flags in their lapels. Wilson stepped before them and declared:

> The present German submarine warfare against commerce is a war against mankind. It is a war against all nations. . . . We are accepting this challenge. . . . We are glad . . . to fight . . . for the ultimate peace of the world. . . . The world must be made safe for democracy.[1]

Wilson asked Congress to declare war on Germany. In the midnight hours of April 5 to 6, the Senate voted 82 to 6 to declare war. In the House of Representatives

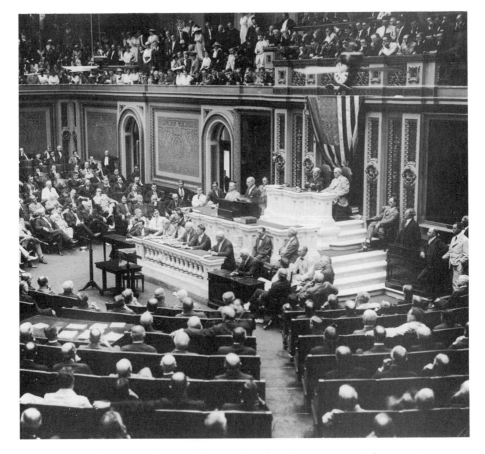

President Woodrow Wilson addresses Congress on February 3, 1917. In his speech Wilson announced that the United States was breaking diplomatic relations with Germany.

the vote for war was 373 to 50. Soon the president officially announced:

> I, Woodrow Wilson, President of the United States of America, do hereby proclaim to all whom it may concern that a state of war exists between the United States and the Imperial German Government.

I WANT YOU!

"We came into this war without an army," General John J. Pershing declared, "so now we must build an entire organization." The United States possessed a powerful navy of 300 ships in 1917, but almost no army. In a nation of 70 million people, there were only about 200,000 regular soldiers and National Guardsmen.

The government decided that the American Expeditionary Force would be composed mainly of draftees. The first Selective Service Act passed in Congress on May 17, 1917. Under the act, all men aged 21 to 30 were required to register for a draft. Later the age limits were extended from 18 to 45. Altogether, over 24 million men registered. Of these, 4.8 million were drafted or volunteered. The selection process began on July 20 when Secretary of War Newton D. Baker put on a blindfold. He reached into a large glass jar and pulled out the number 258. The man holding that number in each local draft board area was called up.

Many Americans were eager to serve. "To the youth of America," recalled Lieutenant George C. Kenney, "World War I was the Great Adventure. Very few of them had ever been outside the United States, but now, after Uncle Sam trained them . . . they would have an opportunity to visit France."[2]

All these new soldiers had to be housed and trained. In the summer of 1917, 200,000 carpenters, plumbers, and electricians rushed to build thirty-two new military camps for the recruits being gathered.

Each of the newly organized military units had its own special flavor. Because the New Yorkers in the new 77th Division included so many sons of immigrants, it came to be called the "Liberty Division" after the Statue of Liberty in New York Harbor. The Irish-Americans who filled the New York City 69th National Guard Regiment proudly called themselves the "Fighting 69th." National Guardsmen from the New England states filled the 26th Division. They called themselves the "Yankee Division." The 42nd Division was made up of men from twenty-six different states and the District of Columbia. One of its officers, Douglas MacArthur, suggested it be named the "Rainbow Division." "It will stretch across the nation like a rainbow," he proudly noted.

The typical recruit was between the ages of 21 and 23 and a bachelor. He stood 5' 7½" tall and weighed around 141 pounds. His uniform was made of drab olive wool. It consisted of a high collared blouse, trousers, a broad-brimmed peaked campaign hat, and leggings that wrapped from ankle to shin. For the recruits, drill, field work, inspection, and reviews filled six days every week. Until there were enough rifles to go around, many men drilled with broomsticks. At Fort Sheridan, Illinois, recruit Frederick T. Edwards wrote to his sister: "We get

At Camp Wadsworth, South Carolina, recruits learn how to scale a wall. At military camps across the United States new soldiers hiked and drilled from dawn to dusk. "Getting ready for war isn't all brass buttons and cheering," one tired young soldier wrote home.

up at 5:15; and from then, until ten o'clock at night every hour is taken." Recruit Samuel M. Wilson later declared, "We drilled and fought dummies with bayonets until we couldn't see straight."

"You can bet we drilled those men hard," recalled Lieutenant Mark Clark. "I drilled them, hiked them, ran them; believe me, every minute for months we were on them. I didn't want to lose any lives because they weren't tough enough."

War Work

"It is not an army that we must shape and train for war. It is a nation," declared Woodrow Wilson. In 1917 the U.S. Army possessed only 285,000 Springfield rifles, about 400 pieces of field artillery, and fewer than 1,500 machine guns. The aviation section of the Army Signal Corps possessed 55 out-of-date biplanes.

Bond-drive posters crying "Buy Liberty Bonds!" were everywhere, persuading citizens to contribute to the war effort. The purchases of Liberty Bonds, Victory Bonds, war savings certificates, and thrift stamps raised $23 billion. Film stars such as Douglas Fairbanks, Sr., Mary Pickford, and Charlie Chaplin tried to outdo each other in selling war bonds at public rallies. Girl Scouts collected peach stones to be burned and made into charcoal for gas-mask filters. Boy Scouts collected scrap metal. The Red Cross, the Y.M.C.A., the Salvation Army, and other volunteer organizations swarmed about training camps, handing out refreshments and putting on church services, shows, and dances.

In a great propaganda campaign, newspapers, books, posters, and films all promoted the war effort and attacked "Kaiser Bill" and the Germans. Americans turned their backs on everything German. Hamburgers found a new name—"Liberty Steak." Sauerkraut became "Liberty Cabbage," and dachshunds became "Liberty Pups." American songwriters composed patriotic tunes such as "K-K-K-Katy," "Goodbye Broadway—Hello France," and "We're All Going Calling on the Kaiser." British war

Douglas Fairbanks, Sr. urges listeners to buy war bonds at a rally on Wall Street in New York City. Fairbanks, Mary Pickford, Charlie Chaplin, and other national celebrities helped raise millions of dollars for the war effort.

songs such as "Tipperary," "Pack Up Your Troubles,"
and "Mademoiselle from Armentieres" also became very
popular.

Americans prepared to send tons of food, ammunition, and supplies to Europe. To "Hooverize" meant to
save food for the people in war-torn Europe. Encourag-
ing wheatless and meatless days was a part of the
campaign waged by U.S. Food Administrator Herbert
Hoover. As early as 1914, Hoover had organized food
programs to feed the starving people of Belgium.

A woman tacks up a U.S. Food Administration poster. Herbert
Hoover headed that organization which sent tons of food to the
starving people of Europe. In 1928, Americans elected Hoover as the
31st president of the United States.

Thousands of American women went to work to aid in United States war production. This worker welds a cylinder water jacket for a machine gun. The barrels of machine guns became so hot when fired that water jackets were needed to keep the barrels cool.

President Wilson named Secretary of the Treasury William G. McAdoo to take control of America's railroads and keep them running smoothly during the war. As chairman of the War Industries Board, Bernard Baruch took charge of many American industries. Baruch, a wealthy Wall Street speculator, had a mind like a computer. Wilson called him "Dr. Facts." "The means of controlling the war effort," Baruch later stated, was knowing "who gets what and when."

Howard E. Coffin, a vice president of the Hudson Motor Car Company, declared, "Twentieth-century warfare demands that the blood of the soldier must be mingled with from three to five parts of the sweat of the man in the factories, mills, mines, and fields of the nation in arms."[3] Thousands of African Americans and American women suddenly found work opportunities they had never had before. The wartime production of United States factories was astonishing. They produced 9.5 million army overcoats, 34 million pairs of shoes, 3.1 million rifles, 5.4 million gas masks, 22 million blankets, tons of machinery and equipment, and great numbers of trucks and locomotives.

Black Jack Pershing

On May 7, 1917, fifty-six-year-old Brigadier General John J. Pershing noted in his diary:

> Was informed by the Secretary of War that I was to command the American troops in France; and that I should be prepared to leave for France as soon as possible.

"General Pershing is a very strong character," a staff officer wrote of the American military commander. "He is extremely cautious . . . does nothing hastily [or] carelessly. . . . He does not fear responsibility."

Pershing seemed the perfect choice for the job. A year earlier, on March 9, 1916, Mexican revolutionary leader Pancho Villa had led a raid into Columbus, New Mexico, killing fifteen Americans and wounding thirteen others. President Wilson swiftly called out units of the U.S. National Guard. A 12,000-man U.S. Army punitive expedition commanded by Pershing soon marched into Mexico to track down Villa. Though Pershing's force failed to catch Villa, the troops got in one year of hard field service and gained a lasting nickname. As they hiked over the adobe soil of Mexico the men often became covered with powdery dust. As a result they were called "adobes," which later became "doughboys."

Born in Laclede, Missouri, and a graduate of the U.S. Military Academy at West Point, class of 1886, Pershing already had earned respect as a tough veteran soldier. In the American West he served with African-American regiments, which later suggested his nickname of "Black Jack." In the Spanish-American War of 1898, Lieutenant Pershing charged up San Juan Hill in Cuba with the Tenth (Negro) Cavalry Regiment. In the Philippines in 1902 to 1903, Captain Pershing led United States forces against the native Moros.

Called to Washington, D.C., in 1917, Pershing was promoted to the command of the American Expeditionary Force (A.E.F.). On May 29, 1917, the British liner *Baltic* sailed from New York with Pershing and 187 staff officers, enlisted men, and clerks on board. After first stopping in England, they continued on to Boulogne, France, reaching there on June 13.

American newspaperman Floyd Gibbons witnessed Pershing's arrival:

> The crowds overflowed the sidewalks. . . . From the . . . balconies and windows overlooking the route, women and children tossed down showers of flowers and bits of colored cloth. . . . Old gray-haired fathers of French fighting men bared their heads and with tears steaming down their cheeks shouted greetings to the tall, thin, gray-mustached American commander who was leading new armies to the support of their sons.[4]

To The Front

"We want men, men, men," French marshal Joffre plainly told the United States. With basic training hardly completed, American soldiers traveled from all across the United States to New York since most of the soldiers left the country from there. All along the railway tracks people waved flags and cheered as troop trains roared past. In New York harbor, soldiers with full packs moved steadily up ship gangplanks. Private William H. Houghton's ship was the U.S.S. *George Washington.* He never forgot leaving the harbor. "I stood on deck watching America disappear from view," he later remarked. "It was the first time in my life I'd been out of sight of land."

Sergeant George Krahnert remembered his crossing with the 1st Division in June 1917: "I was on the *San Jacinto.* . . . We were packed like sardines. You couldn't have fit . . . more troops on her if you used a shoehorn." Aboard the British ship *Justian,* Corporal Michael Shallin recalled, "It was hardly a joy ride. It seems all they kept feeding us was rabbit stew, and I swear, it still had the fur on it." The largest troop ship was the *Leviathan*. In ten trips, the *Leviathan* carried 96,804 soldiers to Europe.

German submarines posed a very real danger during these Atlantic crossings. In March and April of 1917, more than a million tons of British and neutral shipping had been sunk. Britain's Admiral Sir John Jellicoe exclaimed, "It is impossible for us to go on with the war if losses like this continue."[5]

But the Allies soon learned how to combat the U-boat menace. They ran merchant ships across the Atlantic in convoys. In these convoys, dozens of ships sailing together were protected by circling navy destroyers. The destroyers dropped newly developed depth charges (300-pound cans of the explosive TNT) upon the submerged submarines they chased. By September 17, 1917, shipping losses to enemy submarines had fallen to 1 percent.

Pershing and his staff developed the Services of Supply (SOS) to feed and supply the "Yanks" arriving in France. In France, the SOS built its own dock facilities at various French ports, laid a thousand miles of railroad, put up refrigeration and baking plants, and even built candy factories.

America's first troops arrived at Saint-Nazaire, France, at the end of June 1917. These 14,000 men included the army's 1st Division and a regiment of Marines. "They are sturdy rookies," commented Pershing. "We shall make great soldiers of them." One battalion from the 1st Division paraded through Paris on

July 4, 1917. "Vive les Americains!" shouted the French as bands blared military tunes. Excited men and women hugged and kissed these first American soldiers. Pershing remembered seeing "many women forcing their way into the ranks and swinging along arm in arm with the men. With wreaths about their necks and bouquets in their hats and rifles, the column looked like a moving flower garden."

The ceremonies that 4th of July included a visit to Picpus Cemetery in Paris, the burial place of the Marquis de

Soldiers crammed aboard the U.S. Transport *Hancock* wave farewell to the United States. Eighty percent of the troops leaving for Europe sailed out of New York harbor. Most of the others left from Newport News, Virginia.

Lafayette. In 1777, during the American Revolution, the young Lafayette had sailed to America at his own expense and had served bravely in the Continental Army as a major general under General George Washington. Americans felt they owed a debt to such a hero. Standing before his tomb, Lieutenant Colonel Charles E. Stanton of the United States solemnly proclaimed, "Lafayette, we are here!"

In September 1917, Pershing established his headquarters at Chaumont near the Marne River. There he set about building America's army in Europe. American staff officer colonel Charles Dawes declared, "Pershing is the man for this great emergency. He has an immense faculty for disposing of things. He is not only a great soldier, but he has great common sense and tremendous energy."

The U.S.S. *Allen* serves as a convoy ship to help protect the giant troopship *Leviathan* (in the background). The average voyage across the Atlantic took just under eight days.

"We are all working very hard here in France," wrote Pershing, "trying to get things in shape for the large part we are to play in this great war drama." The 26th Division arrived in September. A brigade of Marines and several army units also arrived that month, and they were formed into the new 2nd Division. In October 1917, soldiers of the 42nd Division stepped ashore in France. The Americans were arriving just as fast as they could. Once they landed at French ports, the Yanks piled onto "40 and 8s," French railroad cars designed to hold forty soldiers and eight horses.

On their way to the front, some lucky soldiers had time to visit Paris. Roaming "Gay Par-ee," United States soldiers visited the Eiffel Tower and the Arc de Triumph. They dined at Maxim's and Ciro's restaurants, and cheered the "can-can" girls at the Folies-Bergere. Exclaimed Lieutenant George C. Kenney, "We intended having some fun in Paris before we went to war."

Behind the front lines, the American troops first trained under the French. The 1st Division built a large, realistic trench complex near Gondrecourt. Veteran French troops of the 47th Chasseur Alpine Division (called the Blue Devils) taught the inexperienced American infantrymen how to use such weapons as the French Chauchat automatic rifle and the British Hotchkiss machine gun. The Yanks learned bayonet and grenade techniques. The French instructors also showed how to use flamethrowers and explained how to defend against gas attacks.

At last the time arrived for the American divisions to

fill places in the Allied battle line. Marine corporal J. E. Rendinell never forgot traveling by truck toward the front: "The people in these small villages ran out [and] yelled 'The Americans are coming.' . . . Children were yelling 'Vive l'Amerique.' "

First Blood

After training through the summer, the U.S. 1st Division was the first American unit to reach the front lines. On October 23, 1917, a battery from the 6th Field Artillery of the 1st Division was stationed temporarily in the Toul section of the battle line. They fired the first U.S. Army cannon of the war. Sergeant Alex Arch pulled the lanyard and sent the shell soaring.

On November 2 near midnight, a little over a week later, the Germans staged a trench raid in the same section. German mortar shells smashed into the American line, and machine guns spit streams of bullets toward the Yankee trenches. In the confusion, a German assault company cut through the barbed wire without being discovered. The raiders slipped into an American trench, did their bloody work, and got away, all within ten minutes. "The enemy was very good in hand-to-hand fighting," reported the German lieutenant who led the raid. The Germans left behind three of their own dead and took eleven prisoners. They also killed three Americans. Corporal James B. Gresham, Private Thomas F. Enright, and Private Merle D. Hay were the first Americans killed in the war.

On the night of April 20–21, 1918, the Germans

A poster urging Americans to help finance the war. By 1917 the Germans on the Western Front were battle-hardened veterans. The first American soldiers in France soon tested their courage against such tough troops.

staged a surprise raid on a quiet training area in the Lorraine region. At the village of Seicheprey about 3,000 German shock troops fell on three companies of about 600 men of the American 26th Division. The Yanks fought hard. Major George Rau of the 102nd Infantry Battalion ordered his cooks, truck drivers, and other arriving reinforcements into the fight. In the end the Germans inflicted some 650 casualties, including 81 killed. The Germans used their small victory at Seicheprey as propaganda. Soon afterwards German airplanes dropped photographs of captured American troops along the Allied lines. "Are these the men who are going to save the war for you?" the captions taunted.[6]

The Americans staged their first attack on the enemy on May 28, 1918. Advancing under a heavy artillery barrage, about 4,000 Yanks of the 1st Division commanded by Major General Robert Lee Bullard stormed the village of Cantigny. Before the Germans could prepare their machine guns, the Americans rushed into the streets. They bayoneted Germans in their trenches and hurled grenades. Flamethrowers sprayed liquid fire into enemy dugouts. American lieutenant Clarence R. Huebner remembered seeing one burned German. He "ran ten to fifteen yards then fell over singed to death."

The Yanks captured the town, and fought off German counterattacks over the next three days. Altogether the Germans suffered some 1,600 killed, wounded, and captured in the bloody struggle at Cantigny. The Americans suffered 1,067 casualties. But they had proved that they could fight.

I have a rendezvous with Death
At some disputed barricade,
When spring comes back with rustling shade
And apple blossoms fill the air . . .
    —American poet and soldier Alan Seeger

4 Rendezvous with Death

In the spring of 1918, American troops thrust themselves full force into the nightmare that was World War I. In the following months, battles at Belleau Wood, the Marne, and Saint-Mihiel would write bloody pages in our nation's history book.

Life in the Trenches

American troops began reaching the Western Front in great numbers during the first months of 1918. In the Picardy sector, the American 1st Division began their life in the trenches. The deep trenches were wickered and sandbagged, and long crosscuts were added to prevent damage by shell bursts and mortar fire. Most trenches were deeper than a man's height and about a yard wide. The walls were reinforced by a kind of fence work made

by interlacing wooden sticks. "Duck boards," a kind of
wooden sidewalk, stretched along the bottom to make
walking easier.

The soldiers rose at dawn and breakfasted on hard-
tack crackers, bacon, and coffee. Rolling kitchens behind
the lines prepared hot food and sent it up. Cooks made
mush from cornmeal and fried tinned salmon, which
they called "goldfish." The soldiers called beef stew
"slumgullion" and the stringy corned beef they ate
"monkey meat."

During the winter months of 1918 the Western
Front experienced no great battles. Poisonous gas clouds
sometimes drifted over. The night skies over the muddy,
shell-cratered middle ground often glowed with artillery
fireworks. Soldiers were killed or wounded by snipers
while on guard duty. At night, patrols crawled out into
No-Man's-Land to listen for any enemy activity. Sergeant Merritt D. Cutler of the 27th Division later
remembered, "it was frightening to realize that you were
only fifty to a hundred yards away from some men
whose main aim was to kill you."

Sergeant Earl Goldsmith of the 32nd Division found
one way to fight off boredom. "Most of the time our
biggest excitement was rat shooting," he recalled. "God,
were they big! Some looked like small dogs." Private
Philip H. Hammerslough remembered the filth of the
trenches.

> Each trench section had dugouts with bunks.
> You'd take your turn standing in the trenches,
> then go back into the dugouts. The bunks were all

A wounded Marine lies at the bottom of a muddy trench. "The living conditions weren't any bargain," remembered one American soldier. "Our trenches were only about four feet deep. . . . We had . . . no protection from the rain, and no real communication with headquarters."

full of cooties. During . . . six weeks I never took a
bath. . . . When we left that area, . . . they took us
to this medical center where they . . . took all our
cruddy clothing and burned it. Did it stink!

Most soldiers found the gas mask with its nose
clamp, mouthpiece, and clouding goggles very uncom-
fortable, but necessary. Medical officer Bernard J.
Gallagher, an American fighting with the British, survived one gas attack. "I must have inhaled a lot of gas,"
he later explained. "I suddenly found myself on my back,
gasping for breath, unable to get any air into my lungs,
and deathly sick at my stomach. I was able to get my gas
mask on, and a few whiffs of air through that put me
right again."[1] Troops exposed to exploding gas shells
were evacuated in long lines. Like blind men, they
walked with their hands upon the shoulders of the man
ahead, coughing and vomiting, their eyes sticking shut.
The most frightening gas was mustard gas. No mask was
proof against it. It burned through clothing and flesh,
raising painful blisters, destroying vision, and choking
out life.

The constant pounding of artillery shells caused another major battlefield problem: shell shock. Medical
officer Major William E. Boyce described a few shell-
shock victims he saw: "Some of them cursed and raved . . .
some shook violently . . . some trembled . . . while others
simply stood speechless." Sergeant Merritt D. Cutler
later explained, "Real shell shock was the actual scram-
bling of a man's brain by concussion. If you've ever seen

a man actually lose his wits through shelling, you'd never forget it. The poor guys became jibbering idiots."

Living in the trenches between January and April of 1918 molded the Americans into hardened troops. "It was this period that made us tough," declared Marine sergeant Gerald C. Thomas. "We got tough, we stayed tough."

The Kaiser's Gamble

"The German High Command . . . knew the Americans were landing in force now in France," U.S. Marine lieutenant Samuel Meek remembered, "and they had to break the Allies before the United States could throw a million or more fresh troops at them." German general Ludendorff rushed fifty-two divisions from the now quiet Eastern Front to take part in a great offensive. On the Western Front the German Army eventually swelled to 3,500,000 men.

"Michael," the code name for the German offensive, opened on the foggy morning of March 21, 1918. German troops struck at the point where the 300-mile French line joined the 100-mile British line. Ludendorff planned to split the Allied forces, capture the Channel ports, and outflank Paris from the north. The British defenders found themselves outnumbered four to one. The German divisions smashed a hole in the line fifty miles wide and up to forty miles deep. In four days they crushed the British Fifth Army. On March 23, the people of Paris were stunned when the first shells from three enormous German guns called the "Paris Guns" crashed in the streets of the city. Every twenty minutes the guns fired from seventy-one miles away.

At a meeting on March 26, French marshal Ferdinand Foch asked the French and British war leaders present, "Why aren't you fighting? I would fight without break. I would fight in front of Amiens . . . I would fight all the time." To meet the German threat, Foch was appointed Commander-in-Chief of all of the Allied forces in France. "We are ready and anxious for a chance to do our part in the fight," General Pershing had already told Foch. "Infantry, artillery, aviation, all that we have is yours; use it as you wish."[2] There were more than 500,000 American troops in France by then. Pershing agreed that American divisions would take important places in the battle line.

By the end of May 1918, the Germans were heading for the Marne River. Ludendorff hurled thirty divisions against the French line, captured the city of Soissons, and pushed southward toward the riverside village of Chateau-Thierry. The advancing Germans seized 650 artillery pieces, 2,000 machine guns, and 60,000 French prisoners. The enemy was now within fifty miles of Paris and heading toward open, flat country. Only exhausted French troops stood between them and the capital. Marshal Foch ordered the U.S. 2nd and 3rd Divisions up to the Marne to plug the opening gap.

The 7th Machine Gun Battalion of the American 3rd Division rushed into action. After a 110-mile journey that took twenty-two hours in overloaded trucks, they arrived at Chateau-Thierry on the afternoon of May 31. Lieutenant John T. Bissell and fourteen enlisted men hurried across an important wagon bridge carrying two Hotchkiss heavy machine guns. Bravely, they held off one advancing column of Germans. Other arriving 3rd Division troops took positions on other Marne bridges at Chateau-Thierry. These machine gunners, reinforced by French Moroccans and the American 2nd Division, stalled the Germans on the other side of the Marne River and blocked the way to Paris.

Belleau Wood

A small forest less than a mile wide and two miles deep, called the Belleau Wood, stood just west of Chateau-Thierry. Veteran German troops advanced among the trees. They concealed machine gun nests behind rocks and in the thick underbrush. Mortars and artillery were

The ruins of the village Avocourt, France, just behind the American trenches. German artillery shells have pounded the buildings until hardly a single wall is left standing.

set up to fire upon the open fields leading to the woods. General Pershing ordered the 2nd Division to capture the important position. The 2nd Division, 25,000 men strong, contained a brigade of regular Marines and a brigade of volunteer army troops. Nearing the Belleau Wood some Marines met French soldiers retreating to the rear. The Frenchmen called for the Americans to turn back. "Retreat, hell," answered Marine colonel Wendell C. Neville, "we just got here!"

The Germans were very surprised when the Americans replaced the exhausted French. Marine lieutenant Lemuel Shepherd remembered, "The Germans [were] attacking, and we're knocking the hell out of them with rifle fire, which was something they obviously didn't expect. . . . I guess the Germans didn't realize they were coming against Americans. We could actually hear them yelling about it." From June 1 to June 5, 1918, these Yanks kept the Germans from advancing beyond the wood. Marine corporal J. E. Rendinell recalled one German attack: "How we raked the German ranks. We all took careful aim before every shot. My gun got so hot I could not touch it."

On June 6, Marine brigadier general James Harbord ordered his brigade to rush Belleau Wood. The Marines crawled from rock to rock under withering machine gun fire. "I saw one sergeant literally climb up on the top of a machine-gun nest, driving down into the Germans with his bayonet," Lieutenant Samuel W. Meek later exclaimed. "He was shot, but he put that gun out of commission." The Marines suffered a staggering 1,087 casualties that day. But their violent attack stunned the Germans.

For another two weeks the 2nd Division struggled for control of Belleau Wood. They wore the same clothes for weeks, and the shelling never seemed to stop. "Men sought shelter behind half-finished mounds of earth and hugged the ground," exclaimed Private Elton Mackin. "Whole trees crashed down as heavy shells shook and jarred the earth."[3] The men dug shallow foxholes into the ground for protection and half-jokingly called them graves.

"We have Americans opposite us who are terribly reckless fellows," a German private named Hebel later wrote home. Another German soldier, Emil Amann was impressed when he saw his first American prisoners. "They were all six feet or more tall, well fed with red cheeks. They were the perfect picture of health compared to us pale, skinny and hungry Germans."

Gradually, American artillery and machine guns cut gaps in the enemy defenses. Parties of American riflemen began creeping into the wood. Nest by nest, they cleared the enemy out of the thickets. Finally, after a fourteen-hour artillery barrage followed by a mass assault, the last corner of the wood was seized. Trees lay in splinters from the cannon fire. Dead men lay crumpled in pools of blood. But Marine major Maurice E. Shearer proudly reported, "Woods now U.S. Marine Corps entirely." The neighboring village of Vaux also fell into American hands. The cost had been fearful. In June, the Marines and soldiers of the U.S. 2nd Division suffered 9,777

An American heavy machine gun crew fires on an entrenched
German position. "When you hit, hit hard and don't stop hitting,"
General Pershing grimly instructed his troops.

men killed, wounded, or missing. Marine private Mackin later remarked, "All of us were older by a dozen years than we had been a dozen days before."

Fighting for the Marne

On July 15, 1918, German general Ludendorff launched one more massive offensive. Calling upon every German unit and gun that could be spared, he threw many of them against the Chateau-Thierry sector. In front of the strongest German thrust stood only the understrength American army's 3rd Division.

Just after midnight on July 15, German artillery began firing shrapnel and poison gas shells. German infantry started filtering across the Marne River in boats. Swiftly they bridged the river's 50-yard narrows with pontoons. The American 38th Infantry Regiment commanded by tough Colonel Ulysses Grant McAlexander met the point of the attack. At the riverbank, McAlexander's 3,500 doughboys fiercely struggled to hold their positions with rifles, grenades, pistols, and bayonets. Upriver the 28th Division bolstered the French line. The 42nd Division still farther upriver fought the attackers, too. But no group fought as hard as McAlexander's regiment. Captain Jesse W. Woolridge later discovered fourteen bullet holes in his coat. Private William H. Houghton remembered: "the German corpses . . . were everywhere—both sides of the river and floating up and down the Marne." The battered 38th Regiment held off as many as 20,000 Germans and earned the nickname "The Rock of the Marne."

French commander-in-chief Foch quickly ordered a series of Allied counterattacks. The first of these was aimed at the railroad junction of Soissons. Using the American 1st and 2nd Divisions and a French colonial division containing Senegalese and Moroccan troops, French general Charles Mangin made the thrust. On the night of July 17, in a driving rain, the attack began. The men waded through mud up to their knees for several miles. "No battle ever tried them as hard as the night road to Soissons," recalled American lieutenant John W. Thomason, Jr. At dawn, wave after wave of riflemen rushed through wheat fields toward the plateau leading to Soissons. French staff officer Joseph Helle was amazed at the brave spirit of the Americans. "We were quite unprepared for such fury in an attack," he later declared.[4] Machine guns chopped the Yanks down by the hundreds. Still they came on. Two Marine sergeants, Louis Cukela and Matej Kocak, each won a Medal of Honor by capturing machine gun nests at the point of the bayonet.

By nightfall of July 19, the second day of the battle, the Americans had advanced more than five miles into the German lines, capturing the vital highway from Soissons to Chateau-Thierry. But the cost was high. The 1st Division had suffered some 4,000 casualties. The 2nd Division lost more than 7,000 men killed, wounded, or missing. "Battalions looked like companies, companies like squads," grimly remembered Brigadier General Beaumont B. Buck.

To push the Germans completely back across the

Medical corpsmen carry a wounded soldier out of Vaux, France. By the end of July 1918, the Americans had battled their way to the city of Soissons.

Marne, the 42nd and 4th divisions next attacked in the region of the Ourcq River at the end of July. The 4th Division was the least trained of the troops. Some of the soldiers barely knew how to put the bullet clips in their rifles. But they advanced and held. By August 26, the 28th, 32nd, and 3rd divisions also had joined in the successful Allied push toward the Marne. Meanwhile, on August 8, a British-led army had attacked farther north, near the Belgium border. Within a few days the Germans had been thrown back beyond positions they had held since 1914. General Ludendorff admitted unhappily, "8 August was the black day of the German Army in the history of this war." From that day forward the Germans remained on the defensive.

Saint-Mihiel

"The time may come when the American Army will have to stand the brunt of this war," General Pershing declared. "It would be a grave mistake to give up the idea of building an American Army in all its details as rapidly as possible." By August 1918, there were 1,200,000 Yanks in France. More were arriving at the rate of 10,000 a day. Until now the United States divisions had fought scattered among the French and British armies. But Pershing's dream was to command a united and independent American army. The French and British finally agreed.

On August 30, 1918, Pershing proudly took command of the U.S. First Army's 555,000 men along a forty-mile sector that bounded the town of Saint-Mihiel.

American snipers of the 166th Infantry Regiment fire on Germans near the town of Villers sur Fere, France, in July 1918. Allied attacks along the Marne River threw the Germans completely on the defensive.

Within days he sent an order to his generals: "The First Army will reduce the St. Mihiel salient." Where the German battle line bulged around the town of Saint-Mihiel, an American attack was to force them back and straighten out the line. Staff officer Colonel George C. Marshall designed much of the plan.

From flank to flank, 665,000 soldiers, including 110,000 Frenchmen, assembled for the battle. Moving secretly at night, on muddy roads, they marched in long columns to reach their assigned positions. Horses struggled to pull 3,000 artillery pieces and hundreds of ammunition wagons through the mire.

On September 12, 1918, the Allied offensive began. Lieutenant Phelps Harding of the 77th Division later exclaimed:

> At exactly 1 A.M. the artillery cut loose. It seemed as if all the artillery in France had suddenly opened up. The sky was red with big flashes . . . and the explosions of the heavier shells made the ground tremble.

"I'd been out on a patrol the night before," recalled Sergeant Russell Adams of the 26th Division. "I'd seen all this barbed wire the Germans had set up. I was scared to death when I thought what it would be like to charge through it. Then we had that barrage. . . . Why, all that barbed wire just disappeared—t'wasn't nothing to it."[5]

At 5:00 A.M., the Allied divisions advanced through an early morning fog. By lucky chance, the Germans were in the process of drawing back from Saint-Mihiel when the Americans attacked. They were unprepared for

An American machine gun battalion fills the road during the march to Saint-Mihiel. By September 14, 1918, Pershing's troops had destroyed the bulge in the German defense line.

a hard battle. The Americans moved steadily across the broken ground. The first waves overran the enemy front-line trenches, capturing Germans in swarms. Sergeant Harry J. Adams of the 89th Division called into one dugout for the enemy to surrender and was astonished when three hundred Germans poured out with their hands up.

By nightfall of the first day, most of the U.S. First Army had already reached the objectives assigned for the second day. The offensive liberated two hundred square miles of French territory. "At the cost of only 7,000 casualties, mostly light, we had taken 16,000 prisoners and 443 guns," happily declared General Pershing. On September 14, President Wilson telegraphed his congratulations. "The boys have done what we expected of them and done it in the way we most admire. We are deeply proud of them and their Chief." The Battle of Saint-Mihiel had been a great American success.

Knights Of The Sky

"The only interest and romance in this war was in the air," insisted American brigadier general Billy Mitchell. Nothing caught the imagination of the public as much as the thrill of airplane battles in the sky over France. High above the muddy trenches, German and Allied pilots soared at 100 miles an hour, dueling with each other in "dogfights." These warriors of the air received much newspaper attention and became celebrities.

In the early days of the war, pilots served mostly as aerial observers reporting troop movements and artillery positions. Before long they mounted machine guns on their planes and began firing at one another. Some planes carried two men, but the most famous pilots flew single-seater pursuit planes. The British developed sixty-seven different types of observation, pursuit, and day-and-night bombing aircraft. The French manufactured sixty-four different kinds. These new aircraft included the famous British Bristol and the French Spad.

When an aviator shot down five or more enemy planes he became an "ace." Canadian ace William Bishop scored seventy "kills." French ace Captain René Fonck was credited with seventy-five official kills by war's end. On May 8, 1918, Fonck brought down six airplanes while firing only fifty-six shots. The Germans had their air heroes, too. Germany's Baron Manfred von Richthofen commanded a squadron of brightly colored planes known as "The Flying Circus." His own plane was painted red, and he was called "The Red Baron." Richthofen shot down eighty planes before being shot down himself in September 1918. When General Ludendorff learned of his death, he mourned, "He was worth as much to us as three divisions."

At the beginning of the war, American flyers enlisted in the French Air Service. Developing into first-rate pilots, they won fame as the *Lafayette Escadrille* (Lafayette Squadron). When the United States declared war, some thirty-eight of these veteran pilots transferred to the Aviation Section of the U.S. Army Signal Corps.

At their training center at Issoudun, France, new American pilots learned to fly the French pursuit plane,

Captain Baron Manfred von Richthofen, Germany's greatest flying ace with eighty kills. Luck ran out for "The Red Baron" in September 1918. Canadian pilot Captain Roy Brown swooped in behind von Richthofen's plane and shot it down.

the Nieuport. The first American pursuit squadron was the 94th Squadron. On the sides of their planes they painted a picture of Uncle Sam's hat with a ring around it. They called themselves "The Hat in the Ring Squadron." Major Raoul Lufbery, famed American veteran of the *Lafayette Escadrille*, with seventeen kills, was the training officer of the 94th. In May 1918, Lufbery's plane burst into flames while he was under attack. He jumped from the burning plane and fell to his death.

On April 14, 1918, Lieutenant Douglas Campbell scored the first kill by a pilot in the American service. In July, Campbell became the first American ace, with his fifth kill above the ruined bridges of Chateau-Thierry. "Nobody had any plans for tomorrow," Campbell later declared of his dangerous flying career.

The best American ace, Captain Eddie Rickenbacker, shot down twenty-six German planes in the aerial dogfights. Rickenbacker, a professional race car driver before the war, started his army career as a chauffeur for General Pershing. On April 29, 1918, Rickenbacker attacked his first German plane, a Pfalz. The German pilot, Rickenbacker remembered:

> was running like a scared rabbit. I was gaining upon him every instant and I had my sights trained dead upon his seat. . . . At 150 yards I pressed my triggers. The tracer bullets cut a streak of living fire into the rear of the Pfalz tail. . . . The Pfalz circled a little to the south and the next minute crashed onto the ground. . . . I had brought down my first enemy aeroplane.[6]

Captain Eddie Rickenbacker standing up in his Spad biplane.
Twenty-seven-year-old Rickenbacker was older than most American
pilots. His previous career as a professional race car driver taught
him many skills that he used in the air.

Lieutenant Frank Luke of the 95th "Kicking Mule" Squadron loved shooting down enemy observation balloons. If enemy planes showed up, he also battled them with reckless glee. Luke once recorded five kills (two observation balloons and three planes) in just five minutes. Finally shot down behind German lines on September 29, 1918, Luke landed safely on the ground. Refusing to surrender to enemy soldiers, he tried to shoot his way to an escape with his Colt .45 pistol. He was killed.

During the Saint-Mihiel campaign, more than eight hundred American pilots flew overhead, taking photographs of troop movements, strafing trenches, and dropping bombs. Thirty-seven-year-old Colonel, later General, Billy Mitchell commanded this force. Mitchell insisted that massed air power could destroy the enemy's will to fight. By the end of the war, forty-five American squadrons, totalling some 740 planes, were flying at the front. United States pilots shot down a total of 776 enemy aircraft while losing only 289.

Everybody went mad. The men rushed out of the tents and shouted: "It's over—it's over—it's over!" I could hear one shrill voice screaming wildly: "No more bombs—no more shells—no more misery!"

—British private F. A. Voigt

5 The Eleventh Hour

 "Our day-by-day pressure against the enemy brought day-by-day more prisoners," remembered General Pershing. "Our dogged offensive was wearing down the enemy, who continued desperately to throw his best troops against us."

The Meuse-Argonne Offensive

Immediately after Saint-Mihiel, the Allies decided upon one last offensive in 1918, before the start of winter. The new attack was to take place between the Meuse River and the western edge of the Argonne Forest. Once again Colonel George Marshall organized the movement of American troops, shifting some thirty divisions northward on three main roads, at night without lights. Declared Private Rush S. Young of the 80th Division,

"Everyone and everything was trying to get along at the same time." Trucks crowded with men bumped over pitted roads. Soldiers on foot slogged for hours through the mud. "We had undertaken to launch, with the same army, . . ." explained General Pershing, "two great attacks on battlefields sixty miles apart"—and within a period of two weeks.

September 26, 1918, was the day set for the new offensive. Some 200,000 Americans in nine divisions waited on the line. The Meuse-Argonne front was twenty-five miles wide. On the right lay the Meuse River. Wide and deep, the river followed a twisting course between high cliffs. German artillery frowned from the cliffs down on the doughboys. On the left sprawled the Argonne Forest, its ten miles of tangled trees and thorny underbrush honeycombed with enemy tunnels and concrete dugouts.

On the night of September 25 the Allies began their artillery barrage. Over 3,000 field pieces blazed away at the German line. The artillery bombardment dropped 40,000 tons of explosives on the German lines, more shells than all of the cannon ammunition fired by the Union army during the Civil War.

The shrieking, pounding noise and the reddened night sky fascinated the men waiting in their trenches. As H-hour neared, officers looked at their maps, their watches, and their men. They signaled them to go forward. At dawn on September 26, 1918, the American First Army went over the top. Doughboys in battered helmets and muddy uniforms dashed ahead. But in the

Traffic jams a road on the way to the Argonne. Sometimes the vehicles were able to move at no more than two miles an hour. Still, General Pershing shifted 200,000 Americans sixty miles in just two weeks.

dense fog, men stumbled into shell holes or got lost. German guns tore great holes in the advancing lines. One American soldier recalled:

> I found myself . . . adrift in a blind world of whiteness and noise, groping over something like the surface of the moon . . . half-filled with rusty tangles of wire.[1]

In the thick Argonne Forest, the Germans covered every trail and crowned every height with machine gun nests. As they pushed ahead, the Yanks assaulted one enemy pavilion after another. The German pavilions, built throughout the forest, were thick concrete blockhouses. Breaking into some of these hurriedly deserted bunkers, the astonished Americans found bathtubs with hot and cold running water, paneled libraries, and clubhouses with pianos, bowling alleys, and billiard tables. The Germans, undisturbed in the Argonne Forest for four years, had lived well.

First Lieutenant Louis Brockway of the 78th Division recalled:

> The terrain was some of the toughest to fight in you could find. Remember, the Germans had been fortifying this area for four years. . . . The place was loaded with gorges, and on top of them would be wooded areas loaded with German machine guns. It was murder.

The first American goal was Montfaucon, a village four miles behind the German lines on a height halfway between the Meuse and the Argonne. The 79th Division captured Montfaucon on September 27.

At the start of the campaign, enlisted messenger Paul Shaffer delivered a note to a young Missourian, captain of Battery D, 129th Field Artillery of the 35th Division. The outfit at that moment was bogged down in the mud near Montfaucon, Shaffer recalled:

> Captain Harry S. Truman was standing there, his tin hat pushed on the back of his head. . . . He was a banty officer in spectacles, and when he read my message he started runnin' and cussin' all at the same time, shouting for the guns to turn northwest. He ran about a hundred yards to a little knoll . . . shouting back ranges and giving bearings. . . . There were groups of Germans at the edge of the [distant] woods, stooping low and coming on slowly with machine guns on their hips. . . . [Truman] shouted some cusswords filled with figures down to the battery, and shells started breaking into the enemy clumps. Whole legs were soon flying through the air. He really broke up that counterattack.[2]

This same tough artillery officer, Harry S. Truman, became the thirty-third United States president in 1945.

Colonel George S. Patton, Jr., commanded the 304th Tank Brigade. His tanks made a frontal assault on Montfaucon on September 26. Patton had come to France as an aide to Pershing. But in October 1917 when he learned that the Americans were going to have a tank corps, he applied for the new service. Stating his qualifications, he wrote, "I believe that I have quick judgment and that I am willing to take chances. Also I have always believed in getting close to the enemy."

Patton learned his lessons well during the fighting in the Meuse-Argonne. Later, in World War II, Lieutenant General Patton would become America's greatest tank commander.

The stubborn fight in the Meuse-Argonne continued into October. "In the chill rain of dark nights," Pershing later wrote:

> Our engineers had to build new roads across spongy, shell-torn areas, repair broken roads beyond No Man's Land, and build bridges. Our gunners, with no thought of sleep, put their shoulders to wheels . . . to bring their guns through the mire in support of the infantry, now under the increasing fire of the enemy's artillery.

After a pause to rest the troops and bring up reinforcements, the attack resumed on October 4.

The Lost Battalion

"All right. I'll attack, but whether you'll hear from me again I don't know," remarked Major Charles W. Whittlesey when his colonel gave him instructions to attack the Germans on October 2, 1918. Whittlesey commanded the 1st Battalion of the 308th Infantry Regiment of the 77th Division. He knew his battalion already had pushed too far forward on the Argonne battle line.

At 6:30 A.M. Whittlesey's 1st Battalion, followed by the 2nd Battalion commanded by Captain George G. McMurtry, plunged ahead according to orders. The doughboys crossed stretches of rusty barbed wire and passed over German trenches. At dusk the men dug in

Tanks roll toward the Argonne Forest on September 26, 1918. One hundred eighty-nine French Renault six-ton tanks fought during the first day of the Allied offensive. American troops manned one hundred forty-one of them.

for the night on some high ground beside a road. Part of a battalion from the 307th Infantry Regiment and some machine gunners from a fourth battalion joined them. These riflemen and machine gunners formed a defensive pocket about three hundred yards wide and sixty yards deep.

The next morning Whittlesey discovered that his position was completely surrounded. The Germans had rushed an entire division to close the gap they thought was opening in their line. Altogether, Whittlesey possessed only 554 men to fight off the enemy. The major sent a message to each of his company commanders: "Our mission is to hold this position at all costs. No falling back. Have this understood by every man in your command."[3]

Through the day the Germans attacked and were turned back by machine gun fire and automatic rifle fire. Private Omer Richards was in charge of the 1st Battalion's trained carrier pigeons. During the advance he had carried a cage with eight birds in it. In World War I, army units had no wireless radios for communication. They had not been invented yet. Instead Whittlesey sent carrier pigeons flying back to division headquarters with requests for artillery support.

On the afternoon of October 4, American artillery shells began crashing into the pocket. They knocked down trees and tore up mounds of dirt. Hurriedly Whittlesey scribbled a desperate note: "We are along the road parallel 276.4. Our own artillery is dropping a barrage directly on us. For heaven's sake, stop it." Private

Richards clipped the note to the leg of the last of his carrier pigeons, a favorite bird named Cher Ami, which means "Dear Friend" in French. The bird fluttered away through a storm of German rifle fire and bursting shells. It took Cher Ami two hours to reach the headquarter's pigeon loft twenty-five miles away. The faithful bird had been struck by a bullet that took off one leg and smashed its breastbone. But it delivered its important message. Soon afterwards the American shelling stopped.

By October 5, Whittlesey's medical supplies were gone, and about half of his men lay wounded, many dying. Field medics took the bandages off dead men to use on the newly wounded. The troops endured their worst terror on October 6, when the Germans used flamethrowers against them. Jets of flame flashed within feet of the terrified Yanks. The next day the Germans sent an American prisoner to Whittlesey's lines with a written demand that the Americans surrender. "Come and get us!" angry Yanks shouted through the woods at their nearby enemy.

News of Whittlesey's "Lost Battalion" was being sent to the United States. Americans followed the story closely and prayed for the survival of the brave men. Pershing himself ordered that the troops be rescued with all means possible. Two American divisions at last attacked toward the German lines. Whittlesey's men heard the familiar sound of banging Hotchkiss guns and the crackling of Springfield rifles. The Germans finally withdrew to protect themselves. The five-day siege ended on the night of October 7. The next day 194 survivors of

Whittlesey's original 554 men marched to the rear. American morale soared at news of the heroic "Lost Battalion." Whittlesey and McMurtry both received the Medal of Honor for their fearless leadership.

Sergeant York

French marshal Foch called his feat "the greatest thing accomplished by any private soldier in all the armies of Europe." During an attack near Chatel-Chenhery in the Argonne on October 8, 1918, American corporal Alvin C. York singlehandedly broke up a German battalion.

York was a tall, thirty-year-old, red-haired mountaineer from Pall Mall, Tennessee. Drafted into the army, York had announced he would not kill for religious reasons. While in training camp, however, an army captain persuaded him that it was his duty to fight.

On October 8, 1918, Company G of the 328th Infantry Regiment found itself pinned down in the Argonne. To relieve this pressure Sergeant Bernard Early led a squad on a flanking movement. Seventeen men slowly circled through the brush until they were behind the German lines. Charging into a German camp, they captured a dozen soldiers who were eating breakfast, including a German major. About twenty-five yards away, however, on a small hill, a cluster of German reserve machine guns quickly turned to face the surprise at their rear. Early went down with six bullets in his body. Only Corporal York and seven other men were unwounded. York suddenly found himself in command. While the others hugged the ground, York took up a position in the high brush. "Thousands of bullets kicked up the dust all around us," he later remembered.

York watched for the heads of the Germans to rise above the machine gun nests. "Every time a head done come up, I knocked it down," he explained. A superb backwoods marksman, York could hit an X on a scrap of paper pinned to a tree at a hundred feet. While the German machine guns blazed away in confusion, he peered down the barrel of his Enfield rifle and sent well-aimed shots into their line. "I would hate to think I missed any of them shots," he declared afterwards. "They were all at pretty close range—50 or 60 yards."[4]

Six of the enemy, led by an officer, leaped from a trench and rushed at York's position. The gun barrel of his rifle had become too hot, so he quickly pulled his Colt .45 pistol from its holster. He shot the charging line of Germans down the same way he had shot turkeys at home. He hit the one farthest away first so as not to alarm the ones in front.

Over the next few minutes York continued shooting the machine gunners on the hill. Finally, the captured German major promised, "If you don't shoot any more, I'll make them surrender." He blew his command whistle and about thirty German survivors marched down the hill with their hands raised. Holding a gun to the major's head, York and his seven American comrades marched the Germans, who carried the American wounded, to the rear. Winding their way back through the German lines, they flushed out other machine gun nests. Each time, York forced the German major to call upon the soldiers to surrender.

When he finally reported to his brigade commander to deliver his prisoners, the general said, "Well, York, I hear you have captured the whole damned German army." Modestly, York replied, "I only have one hundred and thirty-two." York had captured one hundred and thirty-two prisoners and thirty-five machine guns. He had also left behind as many as twenty-eight dead Germans. Alvin York was promoted to sergeant and showered with honors from all of the Allied nations for his amazing deed. He also received the Medal of Honor.

Brave Men

"In the cold rain of the clammy mid-October of northern France," wrote frontline *New York Times* correspondent Edwin L. James, "the doughboys of the American Army again today hit the first German line north of Verdun. Against a concentration of machine guns never before equalled, placed in natural positions of great strategic advantage, Pershing's men drove their wedge deeper . . ."

On October 16, 1918, Pershing gave command of the American First Army to Major General Hunter Liggett. At the same time, he created the new American Second Army under the command of General Robert Lee Bullard. As the October weather turned bitter cold, one million doughboys were now fighting in the Meuse-Argonne.

The Germans put up a stubborn defense. General

49191

Four months after capturing 132 Germans in the Argonne Forest, Sergeant Alvin C. York returned to show where the action took place. At the end of the war, the state of Tennessee gave York a farm to reward his bravery.

Ludendorff ordered German general Max von Gallwitz to "put into the fighting front every unit which is at all fit for employment in battle." The battle seesawed back and forth. The American capture of the fields, hills, and woods of the Meuse-Argonne required uncommon valor. Many brave Americans earned places in history. Among them was Captain Sam Woodfill. At 6:00 A.M. on October 13, Woodfill was moving his men toward the town of Cunel when fire from four German machine-gun nests pinned them down in an open field. As bullets ripped up the ground around him, Woodfill, an expert marksman, picked off the five-man German gun crews with his Springfield rifle. Charging one nest, Woodfill shot down two Germans with his pistol. Later as his men were crossing a muddy ravine, he advanced alone, took three prisoners, and knocked out another nest. Now behind enemy lines, he killed two Germans with a pickax. Sam Woodfill survived the battle to receive the Medal of Honor.

A brigade of the 42nd Division commanded by Brigadier General Douglas MacArthur captured the town of Côte de Chatillon on October 16. "Death, cold and remorseless, whistled and sung its way through our ranks," MacArthur later recalled of the difficult attack. Always brave in action, MacArthur would rise to command all United States forces in the Pacific during World War II.

Twenty-six American divisions were actively engaged in the Meuse-Argonne at one time or another. Cherokee, Apache, Choctaw, and other Native Americans fought

Brigadier General Douglas MacArthur (1880-1964) of the 42nd Division. The man who named the "Rainbow Division" would rise to command United States forces in the Pacific during World War II.

with the Oklahoma National Guard unit attached to the 36th Division, which lost close to 3,000 men in two weeks. They battled at Mont Blanc just north of the Meuse-Argonne. No secrecy was needed by that division's telephone talkers. The Germans could not understand the unusual languages these men spoke.

"If this is OUR country, then this is OUR war. We must fight it with every ounce of blood," wrote African-American educator W.E.B. Du Bois when the United States joined the war. Pershing had made it clear that he wanted soldiers regardless of race. A familiar sight for

An American soldier stands on the crest of Montfaucon. By the time the Allies captured the town, few buildings remained standing.

the doughboys arriving in a French port were the African-American stevedores, soldiers who unloaded much of the American supplies off the ships. Of the 200,000 African Americans who served in France, 150,000 worked tirelessly as labor troops. The African-American 92nd Division fought under French command. Four other African-American regiments— the 369th, 370th, 371st, and 372nd infantries—saw heavy fighting in the Meuse-Argonne. The 369th Infantry Regiment spent a record 191 days facing the Germans. After the taking of Sechault in the

African-American troops of the 369th Regiment stand on parade. These brave men were equipped by and served with the French. Their regimental motto was "Let's Go," and they repeatedly proved their worth on the battlefield.

Meuse-Argonne, for which the entire 369th received the French Croix de Guerre medal, the 369th's third battalion was down to seven officers and one hundred and thirty-seven men.

"The pressure which the fresh American masses were putting upon our most sensitive point in the region of the Meuse was too strong," German Marshal Hindenburg finally admitted. Private Rush Young of the 80th Division recalled, "As we advanced, the roads and fields were strewn with dead Germans, horses, masses of artillery, transports, ammunition limbers, helmets, guns, and bayonets." During a six-week period in the fall of 1918, over one million Americans fought. There were over 125,000 casualties, of which some 30,000 died in the bitter Meuse-Argonne battles.

Armistice

By the end of October 1918, the Argonne Forest was in the hands of the Americans. During the first week of November, Pershing had ordered his troops onward to take the city of Sedan. "Unlike the enemy, we had no fresh reserves to throw in," German Marshal Hindenberg later explained. The Kaiser's armies had been crushed on all fronts and were retreating toward their German homeland. The thin German ranks now consisted of teenagers and men past forty.

Bulgaria and Turkey were now out of the war. Turkey surrendered on October 30, 1918, bringing an end to the Ottoman Empire. The Hapsburg Empire vanished on November 3 when Austria-Hungary surrendered.

In Germany, hungry citizens felt lucky when they could find a turnip to buy for dinner. In the German port of Kiel, the German Navy mutinied and took over the city. On November 9, full revolution broke out in Germany. A republic was proclaimed in Berlin, the capital. German Chancellor Prince Max of Baden surrendered his government to the Social Democrats. "On 9 November, Germany . . . collapsed like a house of cards," bemoaned General Ludendorff. "All that we had lived for, all that we had bled four long years to maintain, was gone."

At Spa, the German army headquarters, the generals told Kaiser Wilhelm II that the armies would no longer fight for him. Wilhelm fled by car across the Dutch border and took refuge in the mansion of Count Godard Bentinck. There he signed his formal abdication as King of Prussia and German Emperor. He never saw Germany again, although he lived until 1941.

Soon German government delegates arrived by special train at Compiegne, France, under a flag of truce. The train of Marshal Foch of France was standing at a siding, and a type of ramp soon joined the two stopped trains. At 5:30 A.M. on November 11, 1918, the Germans signed an armistice document. With Germany's surrender, the fighting was ordered to end at 11:00 A.M. on the 11th day of the 11th month of 1918.

Private Philip H. Hammerslough, a machine gunner in the 26th Division, remembered that morning:

> early in the morning of November 11, I was sitting in this dugout when this Doughboy came running

by yelling, 'There's going to be an armistice! There's going to be an armistice!' . . . About an hour later an officer came by and told us it was on the level; the whole thing would be over at 11:00 A.M. . . . The funny thing is when it was over, there was no cheering or waving, or anything like that—just an exhausted silence.

Along the front, other more excited doughboys set bonfires and shot off rockets. Captain Eddie Rickenbacker, the American flying ace, recalled, "Everybody was laughing. . . . 'I've lived through the war!' I heard one . . . pilot

American soldiers at the front celebrate the Armistice ending the war on November 11, 1918.

shouting to himself. . . . Another pilot . . . grasped me securely by the arm and shouted 'We won't be shot at any more!' "[5]

Lieutenant George C. Kenney wrote in his diary: "November 11—It is official. The war is over at 11:00 o'clock this morning. . . . This evening all the French towns and cities are lit up for the first time in years." In newly liberated cities and towns, French citizens showered the soldiers with flowers. Paris went wild, with people dancing and singing in the streets.

"Paris is mad, utterly mad with joy," wrote an American veteran. "Girls spring upon the running boards of motor cars moving slowly through the throngs." In London, all work stopped for the day. Excited crowds blocked traffic in the streets. Across the Atlantic the first news flashes arrived at 3 A.M. By dawn, factory whistles were shrieking and church bells were ringing from Maine to California. In most cities there were parades, cheering, shouting, and flag waving. "The Armistice was signed this morning," announced President Wilson to joyful citizens. "Everything for which America fought has been accomplished."

The Aftermath

Two million American soldiers were stationed in France by November 1918. The fighting in Europe had cost the world an estimated $337 billion. Without American troops, food, munitions, and other materials, the Allies probably would not have won the war.

Over 53,000 Americans had been killed, 63,000 more died of disease. The count of the dead among the other warring nations was even more horrible. British battle dead numbered over 900,000. More than 1,300,000 Frenchmen lay in battlefield cemeteries. Germany had about 1,750,000 men killed, Austria-Hungary about 1,200,000. Italy counted her war dead at 650,000, and Turkish troops suffered some 300,000 deaths. Russia lost a staggering number—easily more than 4,000,000 soldiers dead or missing. Throughout Europe millions more civilians—men, women, and children—died of hunger and disease.

In November 1918, Allied divisions marched east for occupation duty in Germany. President Wilson sailed to Europe in December 1918 to sit at the gathering Paris peace conference. A year earlier, Wilson had explained his idea of what the final peace treaty should contain. Wilson's "Fourteen Points" included freedom of the seas, reduction of armaments, various territorial adjustments, including the independence of Poland, and formation of a general association of nations, a "League of Nations," whose mission would be to preserve world peace.

At last, on January 18, 1919, the conference of seventy delegates from twenty-seven countries assembled in Paris. By March, President Wilson, British Prime Minister David Lloyd George, French Prime Minister Georges Clemenceau, and Italian Prime Minister Vittorio Orlando had become the most influential conference leaders, "The Big Four".

In fighting for his Fourteen Points, Wilson proved himself to be extremely stubborn. "Talk to Wilson?" Clemenceau raged at one point. "How can I talk to a fellow who thinks himself the first man for two thousand years who has known anything about peace on earth?"[1]

The Big Four found themselves poring over maps, trying to determine fair borders for Europe's nations. Three nations—Austria-Hungary, Montenegro, and Serbia—disappeared from the map of Europe. Nine new

The Big Four (left to right) British Prime Minister David Lloyd George, Italian Prime Minister Vittorio Orlando, French Prime Minister Georges Clemenceau, and U.S. President Woodrow Wilson.

independent states came into existence: Latvia, Lithuania, Estonia, Poland, Czechoslovakia, Yugoslavia, Austria, Hungary, and Finland.

The world leaders also punished Germany. The German army was reduced to 100,000; no air force, almost no navy, no tanks, and no heavy guns were allowed. The German Rhineland was made a neutral zone to be occupied by Allied troops for fifteen years. The German Saar valley, with its coal mines, fell into French hands for the same period. The disputed provinces of Alsace and Lorraine were returned to France. Germany also agreed to pay damages to war-torn Belgium and other Allies as well. The formal signing of the treaty took place in the Hall of Mirrors at Versailles on June 28, 1919. In Paris, bands blared, parades formed, guns thundered, and crowds cheered.

Upon returning to Washington, D.C., Wilson called upon the U.S. Senate to ratify the treaty. On July 10, 1919, Wilson appeared before the Senate. The heavy bound volume of the Treaty of Versailles was placed on the clerk's desk. "Dare we reject it and break the heart of the world?" challenged Wilson. He soon realized, however, that many Senators were against the treaty as written. American isolationists, who wished to keep the United States out of world affairs, were against joining the League of Nations.

Wilson decided to take his case directly to the American people. He started on September 3, 1919, although he was suffering from terrible headaches. Cheering masses turned out wherever his train stopped.

EUROPE AFTER WORLD WAR I, 1919

In less than one month, Wilson toured 8,000 miles, delivering speeches from the rear platform of his railroad car. The strain proved to be too great, however. While he was en route from Pueblo, Colorado, to Wichita, Kansas, the president suffered a stroke. For months he lay gravely ill. The vigor of his mind and body never did return, although he survived another four years. On November 19, 1919, the Versailles treaty was rejected by the Senate. Although the League of Nations was designed to save the world from future war, the United States refused to join it.

Most of the doughboys in France were not interested in politics and diplomacy. They just wanted to get back home. Sergeant Tom Brady recalled finally arriving at Pier 54 in New York City aboard a troopship in April 1919. "People working in the big office buildings waved flags and threw out ticker tape," he later wrote. "Red Cross nurses lined the pier and a Marine Band played 'There Will Be a Hot Time . . .', 'How Dry I Am' and other old songs, and the boys yelled themselves hoarse." Sergeant Hugh B. Griffiths, a machine gunner in the 27th Division simply recalled, "We finally returned home—came back to our loved ones and friends. We paraded a bit. We ate some. We partied much. We were mustered out."[2]

These soldiers had changed a lot during their time in Europe. They returned to a nation that was changing greatly as well. After witnessing the horrible death and destruction of world war, Americans wanted to live it up. In 1919, the 18th Amendment became part of the U.S.

Constitution. This amendment prohibited the manufacture, sale, and transportation of alcoholic beverages. Many citizens disobeyed this law, however. Gangsters smuggled liquor into the country. Some people drank at illegal private clubs called "speakeasys" or mixed up batches of homemade gin in their bathtubs.

Other momentous changes were taking place in this postwar period. In 1920 American women finally won the right to vote when the 19th Amendment to the Constitution was passed. Entering the work force in greater numbers, women also eagerly joined the growing excitement of "The Roaring Twenties." They bobbed their hair, wore short skirts, and listened to the new music—jazz. Americans bought automobiles and escaped their simple home lives, traveling the country. They listened to a new invention—the radio—and as a result the world seemed a smaller place.

Events in Europe also held Americans' attention. In July 1918, the Bolsheviks murdered the Russian czar Nicholas II and his family. Several years of civil war shook Russia, as Lenin fought to create the Union of Soviet Socialist Republics (U.S.S.R.). With Lenin's death in 1924, Joseph Stalin became the Russian dictator bringing harsh communist rule to Europe's largest nation.

In Germany, a World War I corporal named Adolf Hitler joined the Nazi political party in 1919 and became its leader. Under Hitler's leadership, the brown-uniformed Nazis preached German pride, race hatred, and revolution. World War I and the demands of

Corporal Adolf Hitler (seated far left) poses with comrades during
World War I. As leader of the Nazi party, Hitler would become
dictator of Germany and plunge Europe into World War II in 1939.

the Treaty of Versailles destroyed the German economy. As his nation plunged into a deep financial depression, Hitler found his opportunity to rise to power. By 1933 Hitler had become Chancellor of Germany. His mad dreams of world conquest would lead to the start of World War II in 1939.

The United States joined this latest conflict in 1941. As they watched their sons march off to war, many American veterans understood how the young men felt. In World War I, the doughboys already had learned the greatest lesson of war. World War I Marine private Elton Mackin perhaps explained those feelings best:

> We met the war at a crossroad. We were young. Europe had been aflame for more than three years, and we had come a goodly way to smell the smoke. Full of wonderings and wanderings, full of restlessness and spice, we heard [war] scream . . . and crash among the distant trees. The guns around us added to the din and suddenly we didn't want to die.

Chronology

June 28, 1914—Archduke Franz Ferdinand of Austria-Hungary assassinated at Sarajevo by Serbian nationalist Gavrilo Princip.

July 28, 1914—Austria-Hungary declares war on Serbia.

August 1–3, 1914—Germany declares war on Russia and France; World War I begins.

August 29, 1914—Russian army defeated by German general Paul von Hindenburg at The Battle of Tannenberg.

September 14, 1914—German troops advance into France and are stopped at First Battle of the Marne; trench warfare begins.

May 7, 1915—A German submarine sinks the British liner *Lusitania.*

January 1916—British troops evacuate Turkey's Gallipoli Peninsula after failing to capture it.

February 1916–June 1916—Battle for Verdun, France.

May 31, 1916—Naval Battle of Jutland in the North Sea.

July 1916–November 1916—Battle of the Somme.

March 16, 1917—Russian Czar Nicholas II abdicates; provisional government takes over Russia.

April 6, 1917—The United States declares war on Germany.

November 7, 1917—The Bolshevik Revolution brings socialist Nikolai Lenin to power in Russia.

December 9, 1917—British general Sir Edmund Allenby captures Jerusalem.

March 3, 1918—Russians sign the Treaty of Brest Litovsk and drop out of the war.

March 21, 1918—Germans begin Operation Michael, their last offensive in France.

May 31, 1918—American troops arrive at Chateau-Thierry near Belleau Wood.

June 1, 1918—The American 2nd Division begins fight for Belleau Wood.

July–August 1918—The Allies put Germany on the defensive during Second Battle of the Marne.

September 12–14, 1918—The Americans capture Saint-Mihiel salient.

September 26, 1918—The Americans begin attack in the Meuse-Argonne.

November 9, 1918—Germany collapses in revolution; Kaiser Wilhelm II abdicates his throne and flees the country.

November 11, 1918—Germans sign armistice at 5:30 A.M. at Compiegne, France; fighting ends at 11:00 A.M.

June 28, 1919—World leaders sign the Treaty of Versailles, which officially ends the war.

Notes by Chapter

Chapter 1

1. D. Hickey and G. Hall, *Seven Days to Disaster* (New York: G. P. Putnam's Sons, 1982), p. 182.

2. Walter Millis, *Road to War: America 1914–1917* (New York: Howard Fertig, 1970), p. 164.

3. Charles Callan Tansill, *America Goes to War* (Gloucester, Mass.: Peter Smith, 1963), p. 290.

4. Louis Filler, ed., *The President Speaks* (New York: G. P. Putnam's Sons, 1964), p. 108.

Chapter 2

1. Henry Berry, *Make the Kaiser Dance* (New York: Arbor House, 1978), p. 121.

2. Lyn Macdonald, *1914–1918: Voices & Images of the Great War* (London: Michael Joseph, Ltd., 1988), p. 19.

3. S.L.A. Marshall, *World War I* (Boston: Houghton Mifflin Company, 1964), p. 222.

4. Ibid.

5. Macdonald, p. 99.

6. Ibid, p. 155.

7. Marshall, p. 287.

8. Ibid., p. 333.

Chapter 3

1. William A. DeGregorio, *The Complete Book of U.S. Presidents* (New York: Dember Books, 1984), p. 424.

2. General George C. Kenney, "A Flier's Journal," *American Heritage*, (December 1969), p. 46.

3. Edward M. Coffman, *The War to End All Wars* (Madison, Wis.: The University of Wisconsin Press, 1986), p. 15.

4. Editors of the *Army Times, The Yanks Are Coming* (New York, G. P. Putnam's Sons, 1960), p. 62.

5. A.J.P. Taylor, *The First World War* (Harmondsworth, Middlesex, England: Penguin Books, Ltd., 1963), p. 180.

6. Henry Berry, *Make the Kaiser Dance* (New York, Arbor House, 1978), p. 33.

Chapter 4

1. Bernard J. Gallagher, "A Yank in the B.E.F.," *American Heritage* (June 1965), p. 101.

2. Editors of the *Army Times, The Yanks Are Coming* (New York: G. P. Putnam's Sons, 1960), pp. 91–93.

3. Elton Mackin, "Suddenly We Didn't Want to Die," *American Heritage*, (February/March 1980), p. 53.

4. Edward M. Coffman, *The War to End All Wars* (Madison, Wis.: The University of Wisconsin Press, 1986), p. 237.

5. Henry Berry, *Make the Kaiser Dance* (New York: Arbor House, 1978), p. 188.

6. Captain Edward V. Rickenbacker, "Fighting the Flying Circus," *The Last Magnificent War* (New York: Paragon House, 1989), pp. 239–240.

Chapter 5

1. S.L.A. Marshall, *World War I* (Boston: Houghton Mifflin Company, 1964), p. 429.

2. Laurence Stallings, *The Doughboys* (New York: Harper & Row, Publishers, 1963), pp. 239–240.

3. Joe McCarthy, "The Lost Battalion," *American Heritage*, (October 1977), p. 90.

4. Edward M. Coffman, *The War to End All Wars* (Madison, Wis.: The University of Wisconsin Press, 1986), p. 324.

5. Captain Edward V. Rickenbacker, "Fighting the Flying Circus," *The Last Magnificent War* (New York: Paragon House, 1989), p. 251.

Chapter 6

1. S.L.A. Marshall, World War I (Boston: Houghton Mifflin Company, 1964), p. 468.

2. Edward M. Coffman, *The War to End All Wars* (Madison, Wis.: The University of Wisconsin Press, 1986), p. 358.

Further Reading

Gurney, Gene. *Flying Aces of World War I*. New York: Random House, 1965.

Hoobler, T., and D. Hoobler. *The Trenches*. New York: G. P. Putnam's Sons, 1978.

Osinski, Alice. *Woodrow Wilson*. Chicago: Children's Press, 1984.

Reeder, Colonel R. *Bold Leaders of World War I*. Boston: Little Brown and Company, 1974.

Remarque, Erich M. *All Quiet on the Western Front*. Boston: Little, Brown, 1975.

Stein, R. C. *The Story of the Lafayette Escadrille*. Chicago: Children's Press, 1983.

Thomas, John. *The True Story of Lawrence of Arabia*. Chicago: Children's Press, 1965.

Werstein, Irving. *The Many Faces of World War I*. New York: Julian Messner, Inc., 1963.

Werstein, Irving. *Over Here and Over There*. New York: W. W. Norton & Company, 1968.

Index